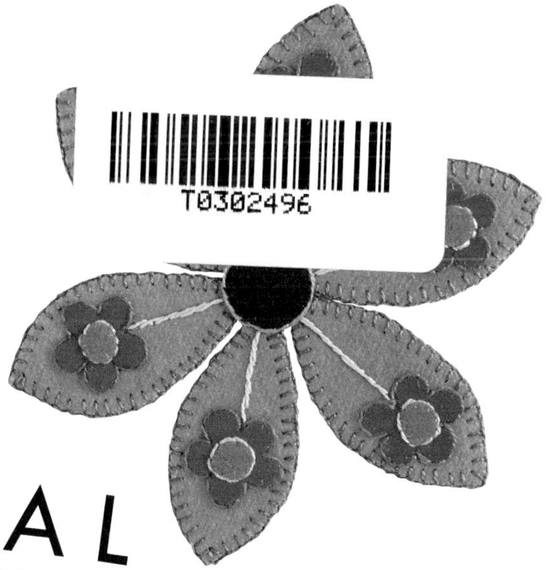

WHIMSICAL Wool Appliqué

50 BLOCKS
7 QUILT PROJECTS

Kim Schaefer

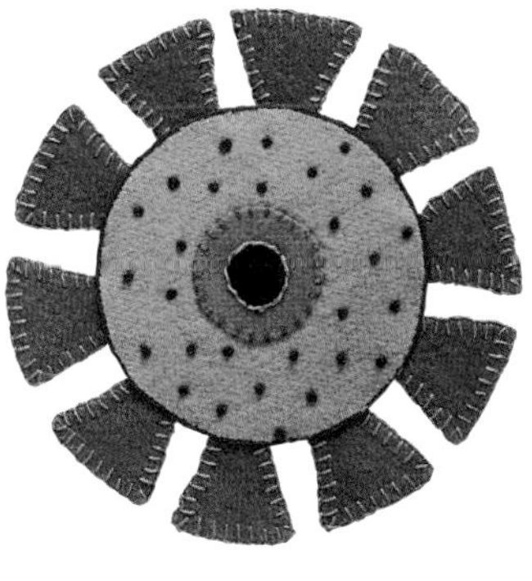

C&T PUBLISHING

Publisher: Amy Marson

Creative Director: Gailen Runge

Acquisitions Editor: Roxane Cerda

Managing Editor: Liz Aneloski

Editor: Lynn Koolish

Technical Editor: Helen Frost

Cover/Book Designer: April Mostek

Production Coordinator: Zinnia Heinzmann

Production Editor: Jennifer Warren

Illustrator: Kirstie L. Pettersen

Photo Assistant: Mai Yong Vang

Cover photography by Lucy Glover

Instructional photography by Mai Yong Vang of C&T Publishing, Inc., unless otherwise noted

Published by C&T Publishing, Inc., P.O. Box 1456, Lafayette, CA 94549

Library of Congress Cataloging-in-Publication Data

Names: Schaefer, Kim, 1960- author.

Title: Whimsical wool appliqué : 50 blocks, 7 quilt projects / Kim Schaefer.

Description: Lafayette, CA : C&T Publishing, Inc., 2018. | Includes bibliographical references.

Identifiers: LCCN 2018003523 | ISBN 9781617456558 (soft cover : alk. paper)

Subjects: LCSH: Appliqué--Patterns. | Quilting--Patterns.

Classification: LCC TT779 .S337 2018 | DDC 746.44/5041--dc23

LC record available at https://lccn.loc.gov/2018003523

Printed in the USA

10 9 8 7 6 5 4

ACKNOWLEDGMENTS

Special thanks to the following people:

Karen Hendrickson, a longtime hand stitcher, for having the patience to teach a newbie a few basic stitches.

Kathy Hall, design director at Andover Fabrics, Inc., for her encouragement and support not only for this book in particular but for the twelve years I have had the privilege of working with her at Andover Fabrics. Kathy is not only an unbelievably gifted fabric designer who is willing to share her vast knowledge and experience with others but also a longtime, extremely talented hand stitcher herself. When I showed Kathy some of the blocks for this book, I knew she would have liked nothing better than to take them from me and stitch them herself. Thank you, Kathy, for writing the perfect introduction to my book.

Helen Frost, my technical editor at C&T Publishing, for once again checking and rechecking the accuracy of my work. I am so grateful for all you do.

Lynn Koolish, my editor at C&T Publishing, for making the whole process so enjoyable and rewarding.

Susan Lawson of Seamingly Slawson Quilts, for her incredible longarm quilting. Susan, your quilting has enhanced all the quilts in this book.

My husband, Gary, for his continued support and encouragement.

Contents

Foreword

Earlier this year, I was excited to hear that Kim was developing a book using wool. As someone who loves to do handwork, I have always thought Kim's designs were perfect for wool and hand appliqué, and I know several people who use her designs for this technique. But what I liked hearing most was that Kim really enjoyed the hand stitching as she worked on the blocks. She is such an expert at machine appliqué that I thought I would never hear her say that. (Most people like one or the other.)

Working with wool is fun and easy. As Kim has shown, these blocks are perfect for beginners. The designs have so much potential for experienced stitchers, as well, who I'm sure will enjoy adding more embroidery, including beading, and even mixing in cotton fabrics to make their blocks unique. I can't wait to add this book to my library!

Kathy Hall.

Kathy Hall
Design Director,
Andover Fabrics, Inc.

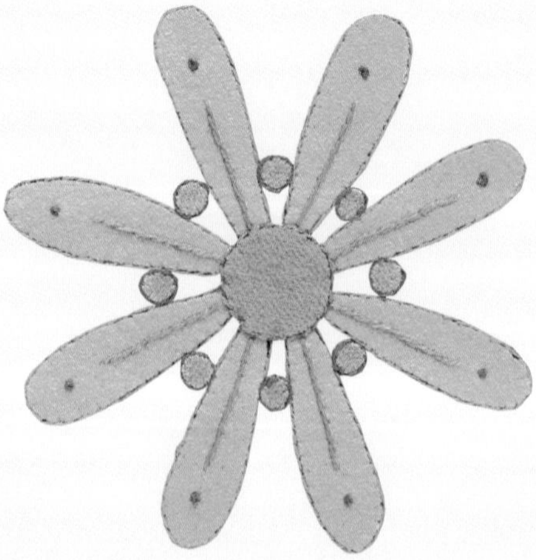

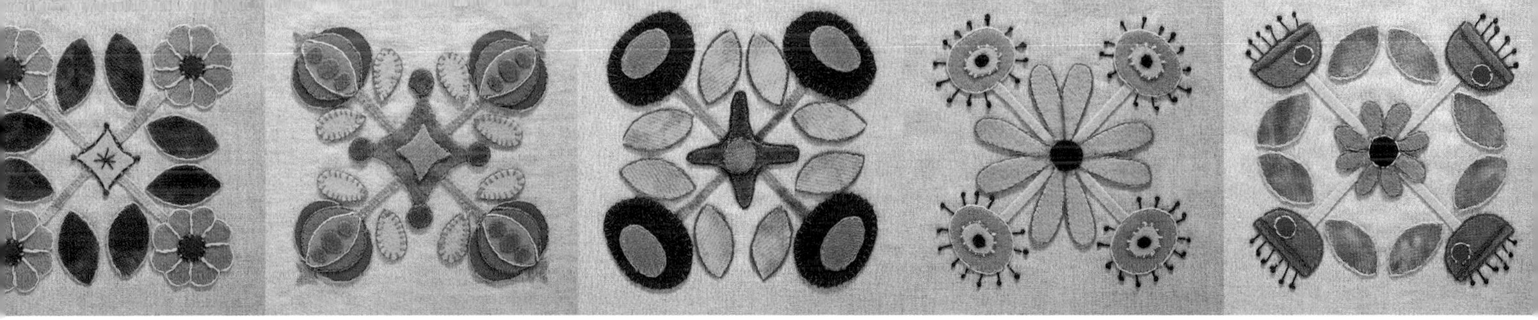

General Instructions

ROTARY CUTTING

I recommend that you cut all the fabrics used in the pieced blocks, borders, and bindings with a rotary cutter, an acrylic ruler, and a cutting mat. Trim the blocks and borders with these tools, as well.

PIECING

All piecing measurements include ¼″ seam allowances. If you sew an accurate ¼″ seam, you will succeed! My biggest and best quiltmaking tip is to learn to sew an accurate ¼″ seam.

PRESSING

For cotton fabrics, press seams to one side—preferably toward the darker fabric. Press flat and avoid sliding the iron over the pieces, which can distort and stretch them. When you join two seamed sections, press the seams in opposite directions so you can nest the seams and reduce bulk.

APPLIQUÉ

All appliqué instructions are for paper-backed fusible web with hand stitching. All the projects could be done with machine appliqué, as well, if you prefer. A lightweight paper-backed fusible web works best. Choose your favorite fusible web and follow the manufacturer's directions.

1. Trace all parts of the appliqué design on the paper side of the fusible web. Trace each layer of the design separately. Whenever 2 shapes in the design butt together, overlap them by about ⅛″ to help prevent the potential of a gap between them. When tracing the shapes, extend the underlapped edge ⅛″ beyond the drawn edge in the pattern.

2. Some pieces are cut as a connected shape. Instead of cutting multiple individual petals, the petals are cut as 1 piece, with dotted lines showing where they connect under another shape.

3. Write the pattern number on each traced shape. The numbers are simply labels for the pieces and do not indicate sewing sequence.

4. Cut around the appliqué shapes, leaving a ¼″ margin around each piece.

5. Iron each fusible web shape to the wrong side of the appropriate fabric, following the manufacturer's instructions for fusing. I don't worry about the grainline when placing the pieces.

6. Cut on the traced lines and peel off the paper backing. A thin layer of fusible web will remain on the wrong side of the fabric. This layer will adhere the appliqué pieces to the backgrounds.

7. Position the pieces on the backgrounds. Press to fuse them in place.

8. When hand stitching around the appliqué pieces, choose the stitch of your choice (see Stitches, page 9). If you are an experienced stitcher, I hope the blocks will inspire you to create some beautiful work. As always, the type of stitching you use and the thread color you select are personal choices.

PUTTING IT ALL TOGETHER

When all the pieces are completed for a project, arrange them on the floor—or, if you are lucky enough to have one, a design wall. Rearrange the pieces until you are happy with the overall look. Each project has specific directions as well as diagrams and photos for assembly.

LAYERING THE QUILT

Cut the batting and backing pieces 4″–5″ larger than the quilt top. Place the pressed backing on the bottom, right side down. Place the batting over the backing and the quilt top on top, right side up. Make sure that all the layers are flat and smooth and that the quilt top is centered over the batting and backing. Pin or baste the quilt.

Note: If you are going to have your top quilted by a longarm quilter, contact them for specific batting and backing requirements, as they may differ from the instructions above.

QUILTING

Quilting is a personal choice; you may prefer hand or machine quilting. My favorite method is to send the quilt top to a longarm quilter. This method keeps my number of unfinished tops low and the number of finished quilts high.

YARDAGE AND FABRIC REQUIREMENTS

I have given yardage and fabric requirements for each project. All the backgrounds in the projects are constructed using cotton fabrics, and the appliqué pieces are cut from felted wool. Of course, you could choose to make the projects using only cotton fabrics.

The cotton fabric amounts are based on a usable width of 42″. Fusible web amounts are based on a width of 17″. The amounts given for binding allow for 2″-wide strips cut on the straight grain. I usually use the same fabric for the backing and binding. It is a good way to use leftover fabric. Cut the binding strips on either the crosswise or lengthwise grain of the leftover fabric—whichever will yield the longest strips.

THREADS

There are a variety of beautiful threads available to hand stitchers. The following are the ones that I've used:

100% cotton 80-weight thread by Aurifil for whipstitching the wool appliqué pieces to the background

perle cotton #8 for the blanket stitch, whipstitch, backstitch, wrapped backstitch, stem stitch, French knot, running stitch, and fly stitch

perle cotton #3 and perle cotton #5 for couching

NEEDLES

Milliners size 1 for French knots

Chenille size 24 for the blanket stitch, whipstitch, backstitch, stem stitch, running stitch, and fly stitch

Chenille size 18 for the wrapped backstitch

Appliqué or sharps size 10 for the invisible whipstitch

STITCHES

To keep it simple for this book, I kept to the most basic of stitches. That's really all you need. Feel free to add any additional stitches that you like. Use the block photos as inspiration for embellishing your blocks. The patterns show suggested embroidery with dashed lines.

Blanket Stitch

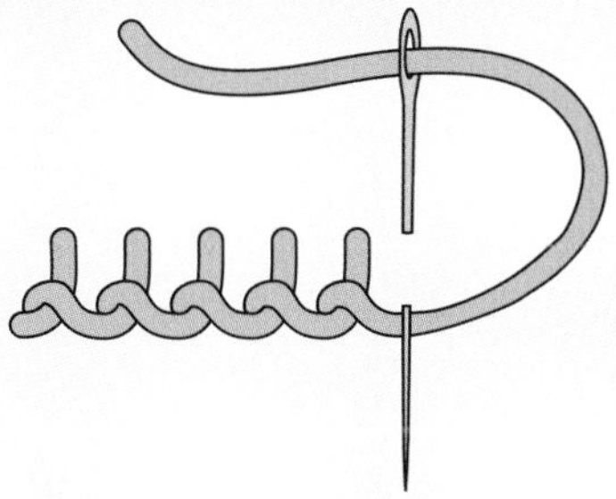

Whipstitch

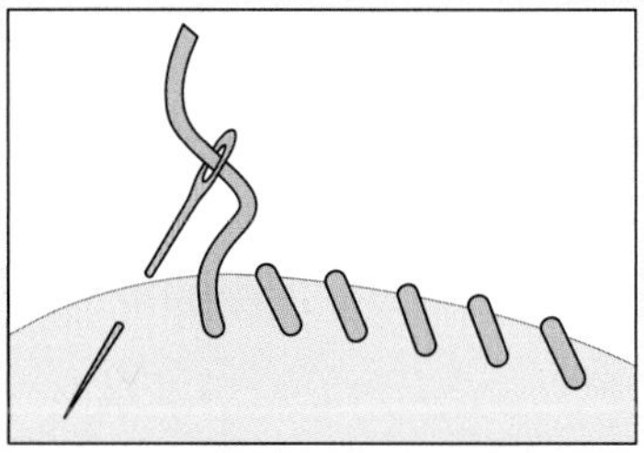

Backstitch

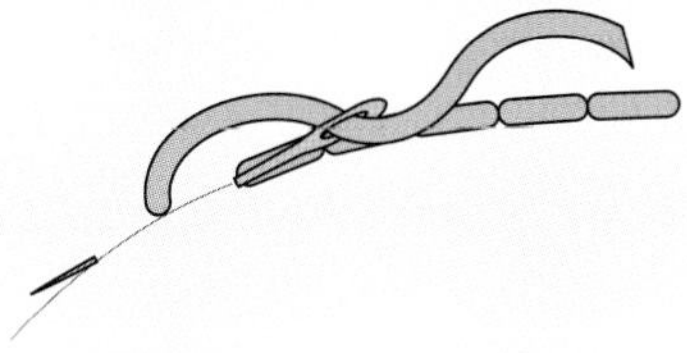

Wrapped Backstitch

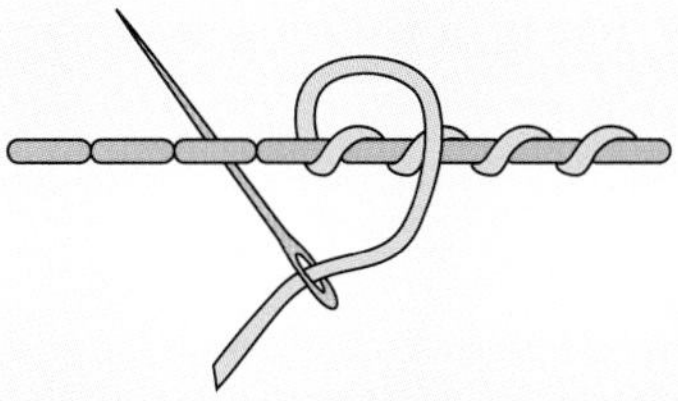

Stem Stitch

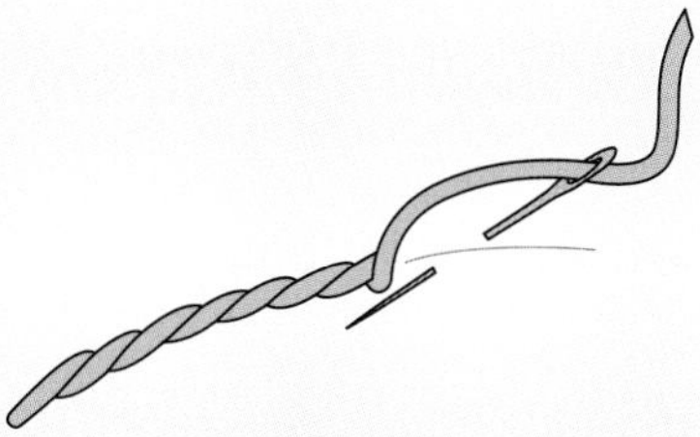

French Knot

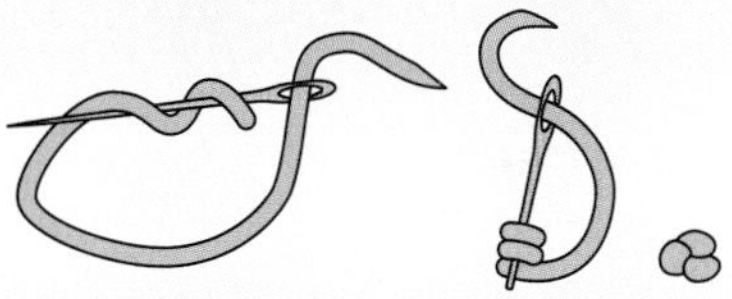

Running Stitch

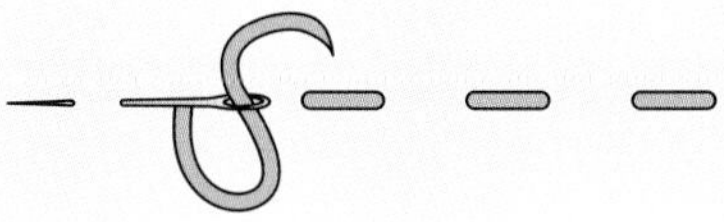

Fly Stitch

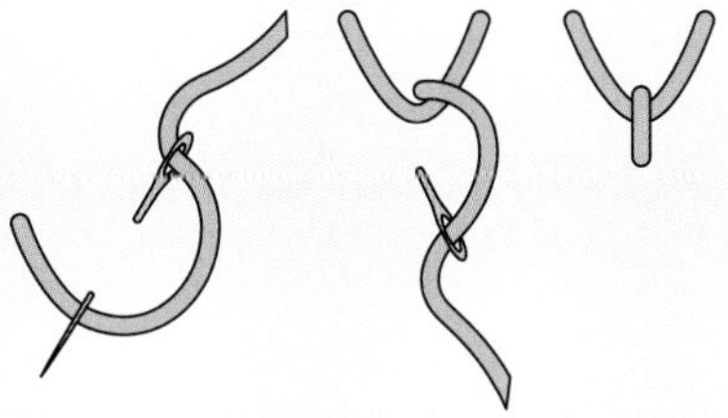

Couching

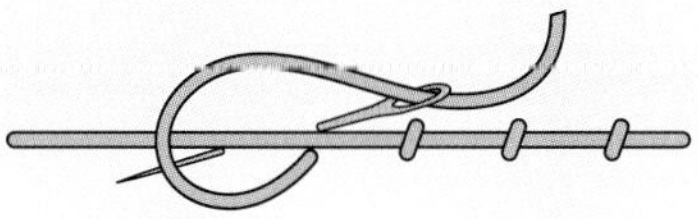

The Projects

Garden Whimsy

FINISHED WALL QUILT: 32½″ × 40½″ • FINISHED BLOCK: 6″ × 6″

I've always been a fan of combining brights with black-and-white prints. The appliqué blocks in this twelve-block quilt are framed by a black-on-white lattice and surrounded by a white-on-black pieced border.

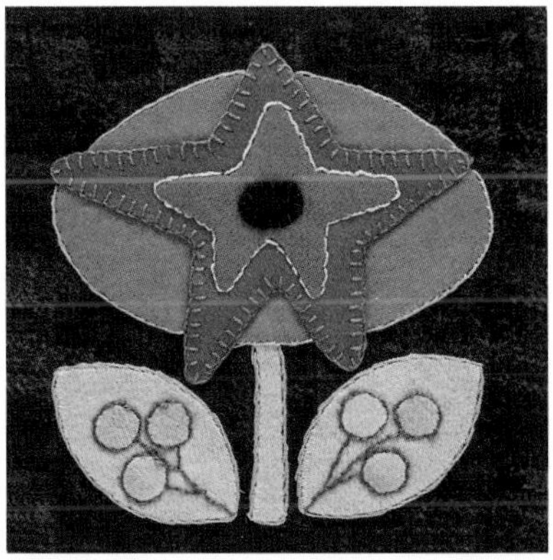

Made by Kim Schaefer, quilted by Susan Lawson of Seamingly Slawson Quilts

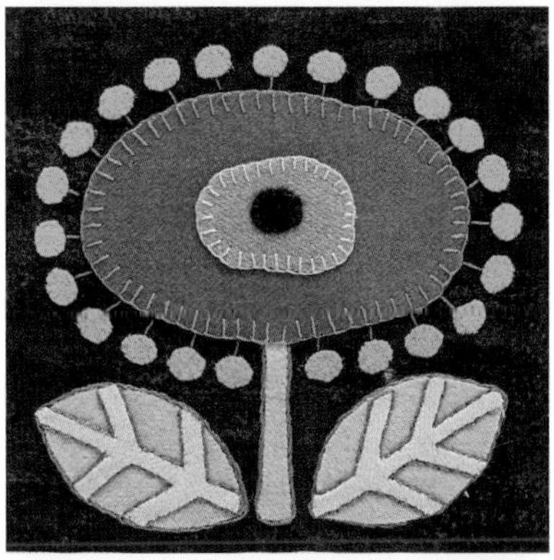

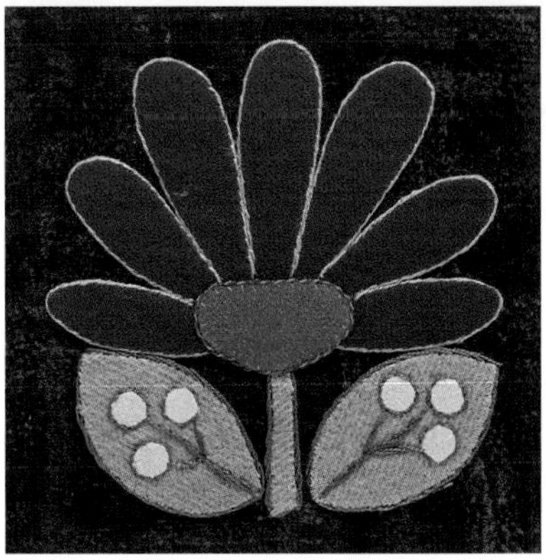

Materials

¾ yard of black for appliqué block backgrounds

⅓ yard of black print for circle square backgrounds

¾ yard of black-on-white print for horizontal and vertical lattice

½ yard of white-on-black print for pieced border

⅛ yard of white-on-black print for pieced border corners

2 squares 10″ × 10″ and 2 squares 5″ × 5″ from assorted purple felted wool for flowers and circles

2 squares 10″ × 10″ and 1 square 5″ × 5″ from assorted orange felted wool for flowers and circles

3 squares 10″ × 10″ from assorted yellow felted wool for flowers and circles

2 squares 10″ × 10″ and 2 squares 5″ × 5″ from assorted blue felted wool for flowers and circles

1 square 10″ × 10″ and 3 squares 5″ × 5″ from assorted pink felted wool for flowers and circles

2 squares 10″ × 10″ and 1 square 5″ × 5″ from assorted red felted wool for flowers, circles, and ladybug

4 squares 10″ × 10″ and 3 squares 5″ × 5″ from assorted green and teal felted wool for leaves and circles

1 square 10″ × 10″ from black felted wool for flowers and ladybug

36″ × 44″ batting

1¾ yards for backing and binding

4 yards of paper-backed fusible web

Assorted threads for appliqué and embroidery

Cutting

CUT FROM THE BLACK:

- 12 squares 7½″ × 7½″ (Trim to 6½″ × 6½″ after the appliqué and embroidery are complete.)

CUT FROM THE BLACK PRINT:

- 20 squares 3½″ × 3½″ (Trim to 2½″ × 2½″ after the appliqué and embroidery are complete.)

CUT FROM THE BLACK-ON-WHITE PRINT:

- 31 rectangles 2½″ × 6½″
- 18 rectangles 2½″ × 3½″

CUT FROM THE BORDER WHITE-ON-BLACK PRINT:

- 14 rectangles 3½″ × 6½″

CUT FROM THE BORDER CORNER WHITE-ON-BLACK PRINT:

- 4 squares 3½″ × 3½″

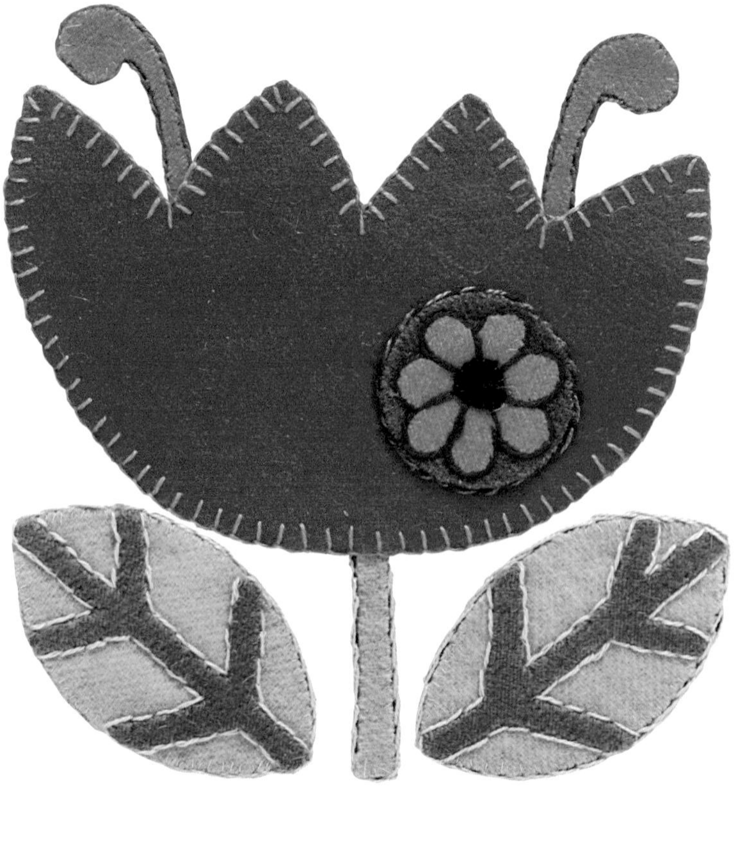

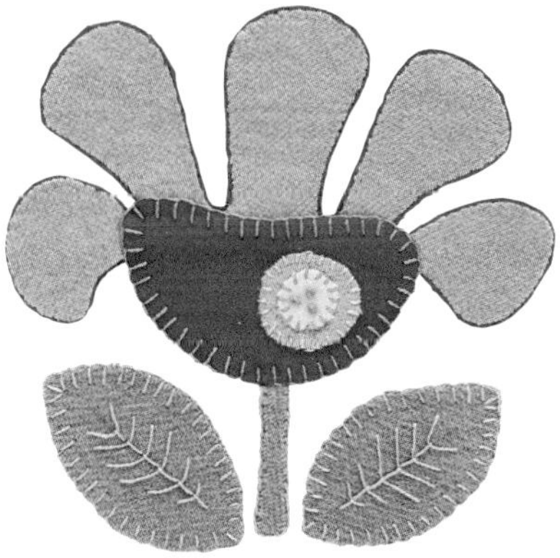

APPLIQUÉING

Refer to Appliqué (page 7) and the appliqué patterns (pages 35–46).

Appliqué the blocks. Embellish with embroidery as desired.

BLOCK A (HAPPY FLOWER)

Cut 1 each of pattern pieces 1–5.

Cut 1 and 1 reversed each of pattern pieces 6–8.

BLOCK B (TULIP)

Cut 1 each of pattern pieces 1–5.

Cut 1 and 1 reversed each of pattern pieces 6–8.

BLOCK C (PRAIRIE FLOWER)

Cut 1 each of pattern pieces 1–5.

Cut 1 and 1 reversed each of pattern pieces 6 and 7.

BLOCK D (MORNING GLORY)

Cut 1 each of pattern pieces 1–21.

Cut 1 and 1 reversed each of pattern piece 22.

BLOCK E (SPECKLED BUBBLE FLOWER)

Cut 1 each of pattern pieces 1–14.

Cut 1 and 1 reversed each of pattern pieces 15 and 16.

Cut 13 of pattern piece 17.

BLOCK F (SUNDANCE)

Cut 1 each of pattern pieces 1–9.

Cut 6 of pattern piece 10.

Cut 1 and 1 reversed each of pattern pieces 11 and 12.

BLOCK G (STAR FLOWER)

Cut 1 each of pattern pieces 1–5.

Cut 1 and 1 reversed each of pattern piece 6.

Cut 6 of pattern piece 7.

BLOCK H (LAZY DAISY)

Cut 1 each of pattern pieces 1–5.

Cut 1 and 1 reversed each of pattern pieces 6 and 7.

BLOCK I (FRINGED HAPPY FLOWER)

Cut 1 each of pattern pieces 1–5.

Cut 1 and 1 reversed each of pattern pieces 6 and 7.

BLOCK J (MOON FLOWER)

Cut 1 each of pattern pieces 1–3.

Cut 1 and 1 reversed each of pattern piece 4.

Cut 6 of pattern piece 5.

BLOCK K (BALL FLOWER)

Cut 1 each of pattern pieces 1–4.

Cut 1 and 1 reversed each of pattern pieces 5 and 6.

Cut 23 of pattern piece 7.

BLOCK L (DUTCH DELIGHT)

Cut 1 each of pattern pieces 1–5.

Cut 1 and 1 reversed each of pattern piece 6.

CIRCLE SQUARES

Cut 20 of pattern piece 1.

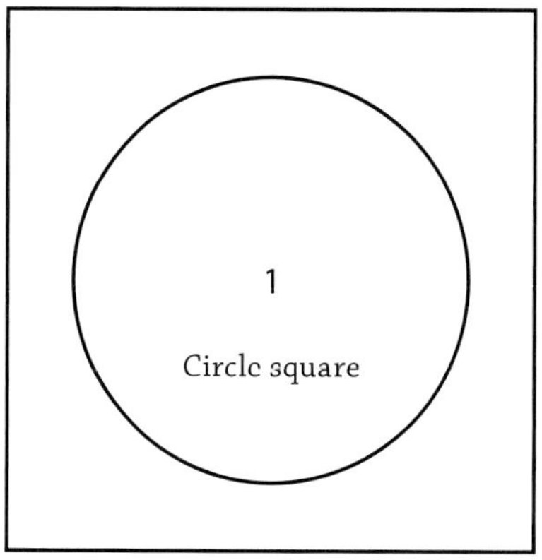

PUTTING IT ALL TOGETHER

Refer to the quilt assembly diagram (at right) as needed.

1. Arrange the blocks in 4 rows of 3 blocks each.

2. Sew the vertical lattice pieces between the blocks and to the ends. Sew the border pieces to the ends of each row. Press.

Piece flower block rows; make 4 rows.

3. Arrange the circle squares in 5 rows of 4 squares each. Sew the horizontal lattice pieces between the squares and to the ends. Press.

Piece horizontal lattice rows; make 5 rows.

4. Arrange and sew the top and bottom pieced borders. Press.

Sew top and bottom pieced borders.

5. Arrange and sew the rows together. Press.

FINISHING

1. Layer the quilt top with the batting and backing. Baste or pin.

2. Quilt as desired and bind.

Quilt assembly

Sweet Tweets

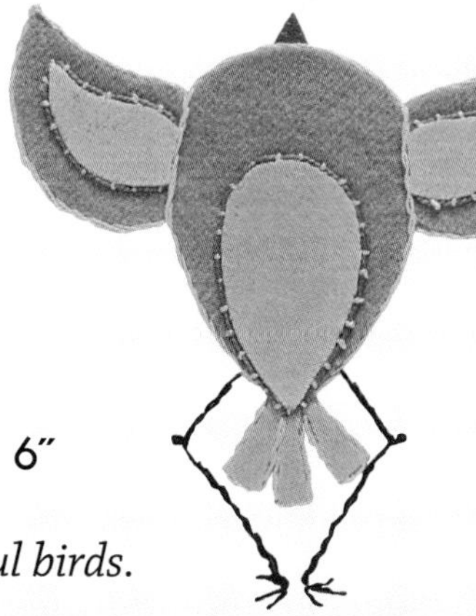

FINISHED WALL QUILT: 36½″ × 12½″ • FINISHED BLOCK: 6″ × 6″

Add a touch of whimsy to your wall or table with this flock of colorful birds.

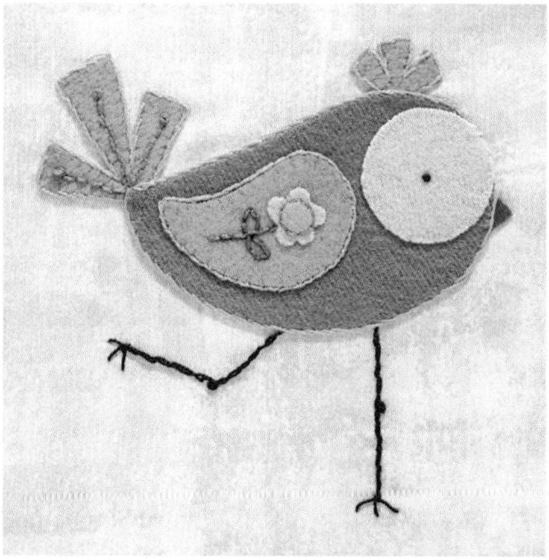

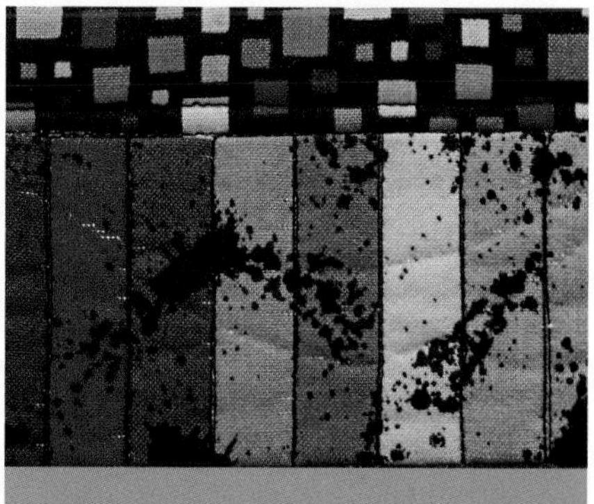

Made by Kim Schaefer, quilted by Susan Lawson of Seamingly Slawson Quilts

Materials

¼ yard of light for appliqué backgrounds

⅛ yard of multicolored print for inner border

⅓ yard of stripe for outer border

2 squares 5″ × 5″ from assorted blue felted wool for birds

3 squares 5″ × 5″ from assorted pink felted wool for birds

2 squares 5″ × 5″ from assorted yellow felted wool for birds

2 squares 5″ × 5″ from assorted red felted wool for birds

2 squares 5″ × 5″ from assorted purple felted wool for birds

1 square 5″ × 5″ from teal felted wool for birds

1 square 5″ × 5″ from green felted wool for birds

1 square 5″ × 5″ from orange felted wool for beaks

1 square 5″ × 5″ from cream felted wool for eyes

40″ × 16″ batting

¾ yard for backing and binding

¾ yard of paper-backed fusible web

Assorted threads for appliqué and embroidery

Cutting

CUT FROM THE LIGHT:

- 5 squares 7½″ × 7½″ (Trim to 6½″ × 6½″ after the appliqué and embroidery are complete.)

CUT FROM THE MULTICOLORED PRINT:

- 2 rectangles 1½″ × 6½″ for the 2 side inner borders
- 2 rectangles 1½″ × 32½″ for the top and bottom inner borders

CUT FROM THE STRIPE:

- 2 rectangles 2½″ × 8½″ for the 2 side outer borders
- 2 rectangles 2½″ × 36½″ for the top and bottom outer borders

APPLIQUÉING

Refer to Appliqué (page 7) and the appliqué patterns (pages 47–51).

Appliqué the blocks. Embellish with embroidery as desired.

BLOCK A (BLUE BIRD)

Cut 1 each of pattern pieces 1–8.

BLOCK B (PINK BIRD)

Cut 1 each of pattern pieces 1–8.

BLOCK C (YELLOW BIRD)

Cut 1 each of pattern pieces 1–4.

Cut 1 and 1 reversed each of pattern piece 5.

BLOCK D (RED BIRD)

Cut 1 each of pattern pieces 1–7.

BLOCK E (PURPLE BIRD)

Cut 1 each of pattern pieces 1–6.

Cut 5 of pattern piece 7.

PUTTING IT ALL TOGETHER

Refer to the quilt assembly diagram (below) as needed.

1. Arrange and sew the blocks in 1 row of 5 blocks. Press.
2. Sew the 2 side inner borders to the quilt top. Press.
3. Sew the top and bottom inner borders to the quilt top. Press.
4. Sew the 2 side outer borders to the quilt top. Press.
5. Sew the top and bottom outer borders to the quilt top. Press.

FINISHING

1. Layer the quilt top with the batting and backing. Baste or pin.
2. Quilt as desired and bind.

Quilt assembly

Snug as a Bug

FINISHED WALL QUILT: 22½″ × 32½″ • FINISHED BLOCK: 6″ × 6″

This collection of fun and friendly bugs are framed by a colorful pieced border.

These blocks would make great single framed blocks (page 29) as well.

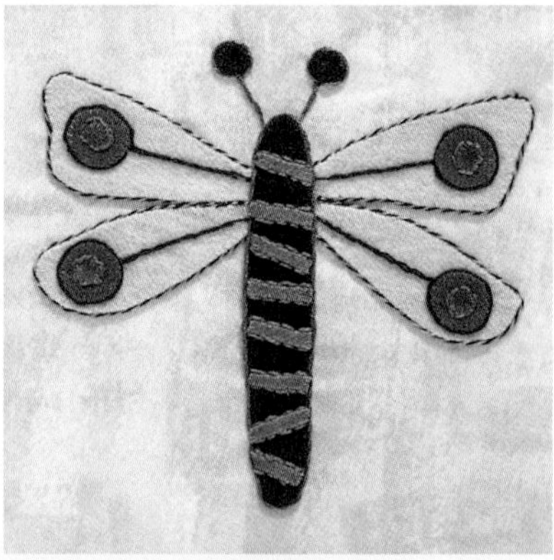

Made by Kim Schaefer, quilted by Susan Lawson of Seamingly Slawson Quilts

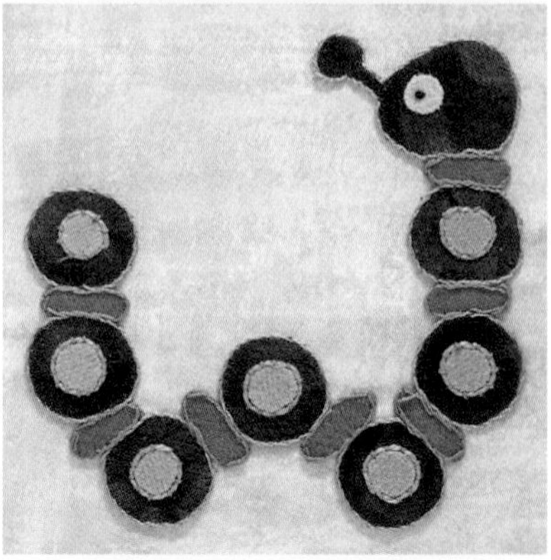

Materials

½ yard of light for appliqué backgrounds

⅓ yard of black for block borders

½ yard total of assorted brights for lattice and pieced borders

1 square 10″ × 10″ and 1 square 5″ × 5″ from assorted blue felted wool for butterfly

1 square 5″ × 5″ from teal felted wool for butterfly

1 square 10″ × 10″ from black felted wool for butterfly, bee, and ladybug

3 squares 5″ × 5″ from assorted purple felted wool for butterfly and dragonfly

2 squares 5″ × 5″ from assorted green felted wool for caterpillar and ladybug

1 square 5″ × 5″ from orange felted wool for caterpillar

2 squares 5″ × 5″ from assorted pink felted wool for snail

1 square 5″ × 5″ from yellow felted wool for bee and ladybug

1 square 10″ × 10″ from cream felted wool for caterpillar, snail, bee, ladybug, and dragonfly

26″ × 36″ batting

1½ yards for backing and binding

1½ yards of paper-backed fusible web

Assorted threads for appliqué and embroidery

Cutting

CUT FROM THE LIGHT:

- 6 squares 7½″ × 7½″ (Trim to 6½″ × 6½″ after the appliqué and embroidery are complete.)

CUT FROM THE BLACK:

- 12 rectangles 1½″ × 6½″ for the block side borders
- 12 rectangles 1½″ × 8½″ for the block top and bottom borders

CUT FROM THE ASSORTED BRIGHTS:

- 80 squares 2½″ × 2½″

APPLIQUÉING

Refer to Appliqué (page 7) and the appliqué patterns (pages 52–57).

Appliqué the blocks. Embellish with embroidery as desired.

BLOCK A (BUTTERFLY)

Cut 1 each of pattern pieces 1–4.

Cut 2 each of pattern pieces 5–8.

BLOCK B (CATERPILLAR)

Cut 1 each of pattern pieces 1–9.

Cut 7 each of pattern pieces 10 and 11.

BLOCK C (SNAIL)

Cut 1 each of pattern pieces 1–3.

Cut 2 each of pattern pieces 4 and 5.

BLOCK D (BUMBLEBEE)

Cut 1 each of pattern pieces 1–6.

Cut 1 and 1 reversed each of pattern pieces 7 and 8.

Cut 2 of pattern piece 9.

Cut 4 of pattern piece 10.

BLOCK E (LADYBUG)

Cut 1 each of pattern pieces 1–11.

Cut 1 and 1 reversed each of pattern piece 12.

BLOCK F (DRAGONFLY)

Cut 1 each of pattern pieces 1–11.

Cut 4 each of pattern pieces 12 and 13.

Cut 2 of pattern piece 14.

PIECING

Refer to the quilt assembly diagram (next page) as needed.

1. Sew the 2 block side borders to the blocks. Press.

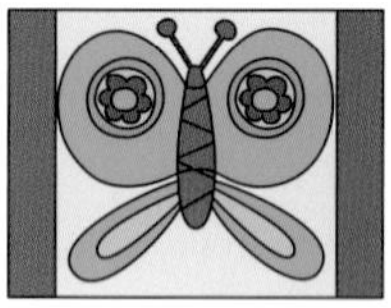

Step 1

2. Sew the block top and bottom borders to the blocks. Press.

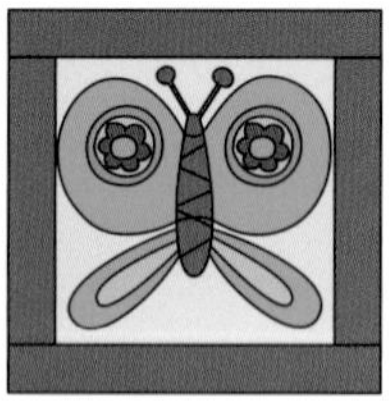

Step 2

3. Arrange the blocks in 3 rows of 2 blocks each.

4. Arrange and sew together 9 sets of 4 squares each for the vertical lattice and pieced border. Press.

Piece vertical lattice; make 9.

5. Sew the vertical lattice pieces between the blocks and to the ends. Press.

6. Arrange and sew together 4 sets of 11 squares each for the horizontal lattice and pieced border. Press.

Piece horizontal lattice; make 4.

7. Sew the horizontal lattice between the rows and to the top and bottom. Press.

FINISHING

1. Layer the quilt top with the batting and backing. Baste or pin.

2. Quilt as desired and bind.

Quilt assembly

Bloomin' Beauties

FINISHED WALL QUILT: 28½″ × 22½″ • FINISHED BLOCK: 6″ × 6″

Six colorful blocks are surrounded by a leafy vine border.

A fun project, perfect for either a wall quilt or table topper.

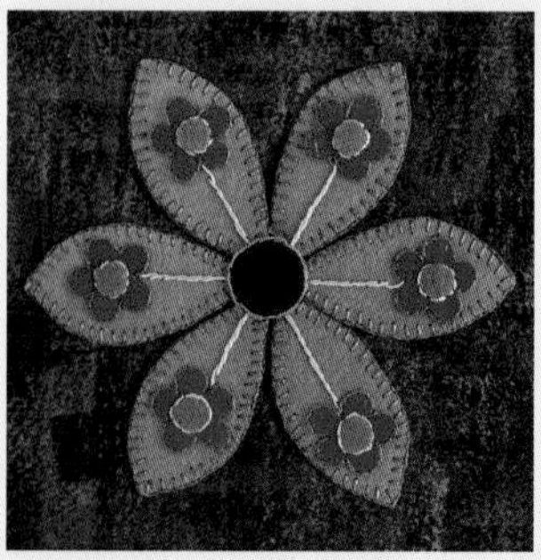

Made by Kim Schaefer,
quilted by Susan Lawson of
Seamingly Slawson Quilts

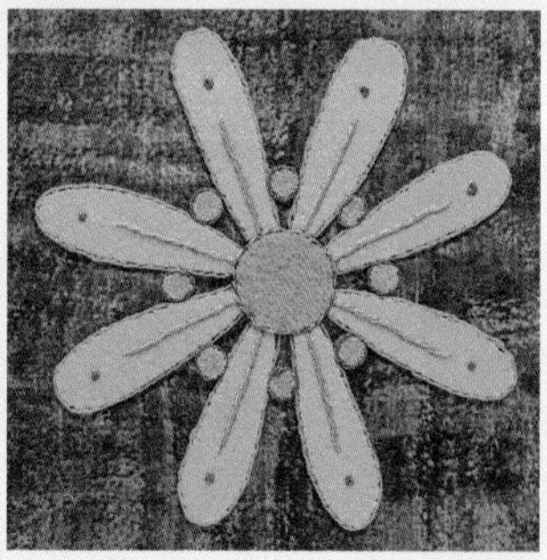

Materials

½ yard total of assorted teals and greens for appliqué block backgrounds and corner squares

¼ yard of dark green for inner border

⅝ yard of black for appliquéd outer border

1 square 10″ × 10″ and 2 squares 5″ × 5″ from assorted orange felted wool for flowers

1 square 10″ × 10″ and 1 square 5″ × 5″ from assorted red felted wool for flowers

1 square 5″ × 5″ from black felted wool for flower centers

1 square 10″ × 10″ and 1 square 5″ × 5″ from assorted pink felted wool for flowers

1 square 10″ × 10″ and 2 squares 5″ × 5″ from assorted purple felted wool for flowers

1 square 10″ × 10″ and 2 squares 5″ × 5″ from assorted yellow felted wool for flowers

1 square 10″ × 10″ and 2 squares 5″ × 5″ from assorted blue felted wool for flowers

1 rectangle 6″ × 22″ and 1 square 5″ × 5″ from assorted teal felted wool for corner squares and vine

4 squares 10″ × 10″ from assorted green felted wool for leaves

32″ × 26″ batting

1⅛ yards for backing and binding

1½ yards of paper-backed fusible web

Assorted threads for appliqué and embroidery

Cutting

CUT FROM THE ASSORTED TEALS AND GREENS:

- 6 squares 7½″ × 7½″ (Trim to 6½″ × 6½″ after the appliqué and embroidery are complete.)
- 4 squares 5½″ × 5½″ (Trim to 4½″ × 4½″ after the appliqué and embroidery are complete.)

CUT FROM THE DARK GREEN:

- 2 rectangles 1½″ × 12½″ for the 2 side inner borders
- 2 rectangles 1½″ × 20½″ for the top and bottom inner borders

CUT FROM THE BLACK:

- 2 rectangles 5½″ × 15½″ for the 2 side outer borders (Trim to 4½″ × 14½″ after the appliqué and embroidery are complete.)
- 2 rectangles 5½″ × 21½″ for the top and bottom outer borders (Trim to 4½″ × 20½″ after the appliqué and embroidery are complete.)

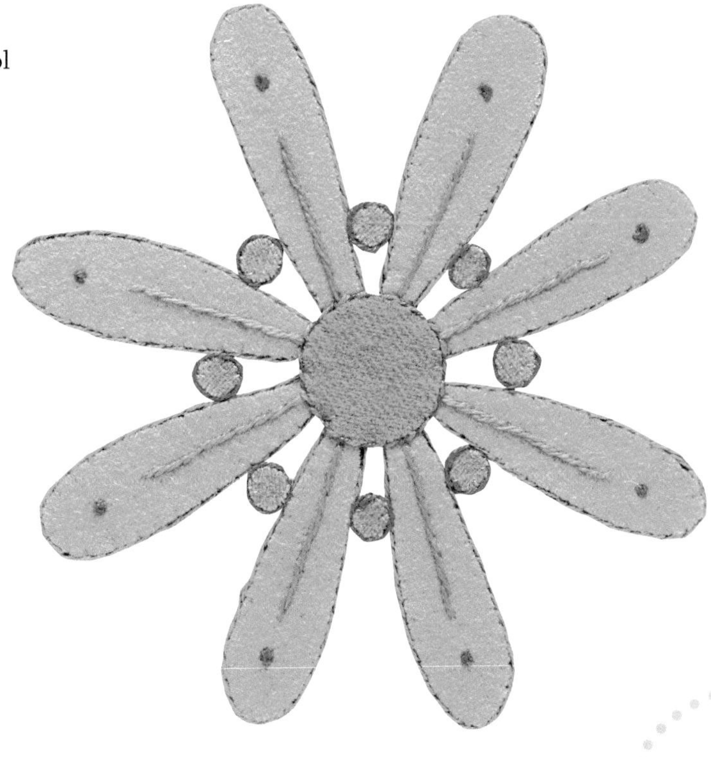

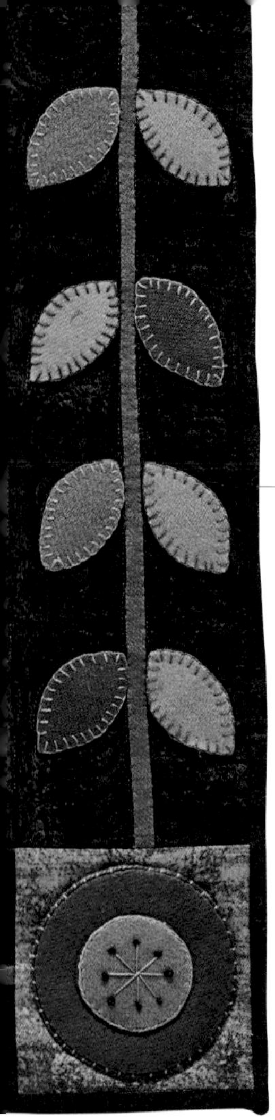

APPLIQUÉING

Refer to Appliqué (page 7) and the appliqué patterns (pages 58–64).

Appliqué the blocks and outer border. Embellish with embroidery as desired.

BLOCK A (FANCY TIPS)

Cut 1 each of pattern pieces 1 and 2.

Cut 6 each of pattern pieces 3 and 4.

BLOCK B (SASSY FLOWER)

Cut 1 each of pattern pieces 1–3.

Cut 12 of pattern piece 4.

BLOCK C (DAZZLE FLOWER)

Cut 1 each of pattern pieces 1 and 2.

Cut 8 of pattern piece 3.

BLOCK D (SPARKLE FLOWER)

Cut 1 each of pattern pieces 1–3.

BLOCK E (BUTTERCUP)

Cut 1 each of pattern pieces 1 and 2.

Cut 8 of pattern piece 3.

BLOCK F (WILDFLOWER)

Cut 1 each of pattern pieces 1 and 2.

Cut 8 of pattern piece 3.

CORNER SQUARES

Cut 4 each of pattern pieces 1 and 2.

OUTER BORDERS

Cut 2 pieces ¼″ × 14½″ for the side outer-border vines.

Cut 2 pieces ¼″ × 20½″ for the top and bottom outer-border vines.

Cut 20 each of pattern pieces 1 and 2 (leaves).

PUTTING IT ALL TOGETHER

Refer to the quilt assembly diagram (at right) as needed.

1. Arrange and sew the blocks in 2 rows of 3 blocks each. Press.

2. Sew together the rows. Press.

3. Sew the 2 side inner borders to the quilt top. Press.

4. Sew the top and bottom inner borders to the quilt top. Press.

5. Sew the 2 side outer borders to the quilt top. Press.

6. Sew the corner squares to the ends of the top and bottom borders. Press.

7. Sew the top and bottom outer borders to the quilt top. Press.

FINISHING

1. Layer the quilt top with the batting and backing. Baste or pin.

2. Quilt as desired and bind.

Quilt assembly

Enchanted Garden

FINISHED WALL QUILT: 33½″ × 33½″ • FINISHED BLOCK: 6″ × 6″

Bring the glories of the garden inside to enjoy throughout the year.

Made by Kim Schaefer, quilted by Susan Lawson of Seamingly Slawson Quilts

Materials

½ yard of light for appliqué block backgrounds

½ yard of black for block borders

⅓ yard of green for vertical and horizontal lattice

½ yard of dark green for outer border

4 squares 5″ × 5″ from assorted blue felted wool for flowers

2 squares 5″ × 5″ from assorted teal felted wool for flowers

1 square 10″ × 10″ and 2 squares 5″ × 5″ from assorted orange felted wool for flowers

4 squares 5″ × 5″ from assorted purple felted wool for flowers

2 squares 5″ × 5″ from assorted yellow felted wool for flowers

2 squares 5″ × 5″ from assorted red felted wool for flowers

3 squares 5″ × 5″ from assorted pink felted wool for flowers

1 square 5″ × 5″ from black felted wool for flowers

4 squares 10″ × 10″ from assorted green felted wool for stems and leaves

37″ × 37″ batting

1½ yards for backing and binding

3 yards of paper-backed fusible web

Assorted threads for appliqué and embroidery

Cutting

CUT FROM THE LIGHT:

- 9 squares 7½″ × 7½″ (Trim to 6½″ × 6½″ after the appliqué and embroidery are complete.)

CUT FROM THE BLACK:

- 18 rectangles 1½″ × 6½″ for the block side borders
- 18 rectangles 1½″ × 8½″ for the block top and bottom borders

CUT FROM THE GREEN:

- 12 rectangles 1¼″ × 8½″ for the vertical lattice
- 4 strips 1¼″ × 27½″ for the horizontal lattice

CUT FROM THE DARK GREEN:

- 2 strips 3½″ × 27½″ for the 2 side borders
- 2 strips 3½″ × 33½″ for the top and bottom borders

APPLIQUÉING

Refer to Appliqué (page 7) and the appliqué patterns (pages 65–73).

Appliqué the blocks. Embellish with embroidery as desired.

BLOCK A (ABIGAIL)

Cut 1 of pattern piece 1.

Cut 4 each of pattern pieces 2–4.

Cut 8 of pattern piece 5.

BLOCK B (JANY JINGLE)

Cut 1 each of pattern pieces 1 and 2.

Cut 4 each of pattern pieces 3–5.

Cut 8 of pattern piece 6.

BLOCK C (DIZZY IZZI)

Cut 1 of pattern piece 1.

Cut 4 each of pattern pieces 2–4.

Cut 8 of pattern piece 5.

BLOCK D (MADDIE MAGIC)

Cut 1 each of pattern pieces 1 and 2.

Cut 4 each of pattern pieces 3–5.

Cut 8 of pattern piece 6.

BLOCK E (PHOEBE)

Cut 1 each of pattern pieces 1 and 2.

Cut 4 each of pattern pieces 3–10.

Cut 8 of pattern piece 11.

BLOCK F (LUCI LU)

Cut 1 each of pattern pieces 1 and 2.

Cut 4 each of pattern pieces 3–6.

BLOCK G (BELLA)

Cut 1 of pattern piece 1.

Cut 4 each of pattern pieces 2 and 3.

Cut 8 of pattern piece 4.

BLOCK H (MISS MOLLY)

Cut 1 each of pattern pieces 1 and 2.

Cut 4 each of pattern pieces 3–5.

Cut 8 of pattern piece 6.

BLOCK I (LANIE LOVE)

Cut 1 each of pattern pieces 1 and 2.

Cut 4 each of pattern pieces 3–6.

PUTTING IT ALL TOGETHER

Refer to the quilt assembly diagram (below) as needed.

1. Sew the 2 block side borders to the blocks. Press.

Step 1

2. Sew the block top and bottom borders to the blocks. Press.

Step 2

3. Sew the vertical lattice strips between the blocks and to the ends. Press.

4. Sew the horizontal lattice strips between the rows and to the ends. Press.

5. Sew together the rows. Press.

6. Sew the 2 side borders to the quilt top. Press.

7. Sew the top and bottom borders to the quilt top. Press.

FINISHING

1. Layer the quilt top with the batting and backing. Baste or pin.

2. Quilt as desired and bind.

Quilt assembly

Ring Around the Bluebell

FINISHED QUILT: 12½″ × 12½″ • FINISHED BLOCK: 6″ × 6″

Single-block quilts are fast and fun. Select your favorite block (or blocks), and make one or make a few for a small grouping with a big impact.

Made by Kim Schaefer, quilted by Susan Lawson of Seamingly Slawson Quilts

Materials

¼ yard of green for appliqué background

⅓ yard total of 2 teals for appliqué border backgrounds

1 square 10″ × 10″ and 1 square 5″ × 5″ from assorted teal felted wool for flower

1 square 5″ × 5″ from black felted wool for flower center

2 squares 10″ × 10″ from assorted green felted wool for leaves and vines

1 square 10″ × 10″ and 1 square 5″ × 5″ from assorted red felted wool for flowers

16″ × 16″ batting

½ yard for backing and binding

½ yard of paper-backed fusible web

Assorted threads for appliqué and embroidery

Cutting

CUT FROM THE GREEN:

- 1 square 6½″ × 6½″

CUT FROM THE TEALS:

- 4 squares 3½″ × 3½″
- 4 rectangles 3½″ × 6½″

Note: These background pieces are not cut oversize and trimmed because they are pieced together before appliquéing and embroidering.

PIECING

Refer to the quilt assembly diagram (at right) as needed.

Arrange and sew together the appliqué backgrounds to form the quilt top.

Piece quilt top.

APPLIQUÉING

Refer to Appliqué (page 7) and the appliqué patterns (pages 74 and 75).

Appliqué the blocks and borders.

BLOCK A (BLUEBELL)

Cut 1 each of pattern pieces 1–3.

BLOCK B (CORNER BLOCK)

Cut 4 each of pattern pieces 1 and 2.

BLOCK C (BORDER RECTANGLE)

Cut 4 each of pattern pieces 1 and 2.

Cut 4 and 4 reversed each of pattern piece 3.

Cut 4 of pattern piece 4 (vine).

FINISHING

1. Layer the quilt top with the batting and backing. Baste or pin.
2. Quilt as desired and bind.

Quilt assembly

Flower Power Pillow

FINISHED PILLOW: 24½″ × 24½″ • FINISHED BLOCK: 6″ × 6″

A single-flower block in an array of colors is combined with a bright, cheery fabric for the lattice and border to create this happy pillow.

Made by Kim Schaefer

Materials

½ yard total of assorted greens and teals for appliqué block backgrounds

1¼ yards of print for lattice, borders, and back

2 squares 10″ × 10″ and 2 squares 5″ × 5″ from assorted pink felted wool for flowers

2 squares 10″ × 10″ and 2 squares 5″ × 5″ from assorted purple felted wool for flowers

1 square 10″ × 10″ and 2 squares 5″ × 5″ from assorted blue felted wool for flowers

1 square 10″ × 10″ and 2 squares 5″ × 5″ from assorted teal felted wool for flowers

1 square 10″ × 10″ and 2 squares 5″ × 5″ from assorted yellow felted wool for flowers

1 square 10″ × 10″ and 2 squares 5″ × 5″ from assorted orange felted wool for flowers

1 square 10″ × 10″ and 2 squares 5″ × 5″ from assorted red felted wool for flowers

3 yards of purchased black piping

24″ × 24″ purchased pillow form

1 yard of paper-backed fusible web

Assorted threads for appliqué and embroidery

Cutting

CUT FROM THE ASSORTED GREENS AND TEALS:

- 9 squares 7½″ × 7½″ (Trim to 6½″ × 6½″ after the appliqué and embroidery are complete.)

CUT FROM THE PRINT:

- 6 rectangles 1½″ × 6½″ for the vertical lattice
- 2 rectangles 1½″ × 20½″ for the horizontal lattice
- 2 rectangles 2½″ × 20½″ for the 2 side borders
- 2 rectangles 2½″ × 24½″ for the top and bottom borders
- 2 rectangles 15½″ × 24½″ for the pillow back

APPLIQUÉING

Refer to Appliqué (page 7) and the appliqué pattern (page 76).

Appliqué the blocks. Embellish with embroidery as desired.

SQUARE FLOWER

Cut 9 each of pattern pieces 1–3.

PUTTING IT ALL TOGETHER

Refer to the pillow assembly diagram (next page) as needed.

1. Arrange the blocks in 3 rows of 3 blocks each.
2. Sew the vertical lattice pieces between the blocks. Press.
3. Sew the horizontal lattice pieces between the rows. Press.
4. Sew the 2 side borders to the pillow top. Press.
5. Sew the top and bottom borders to the pillow top. Press.

Pillow assembly

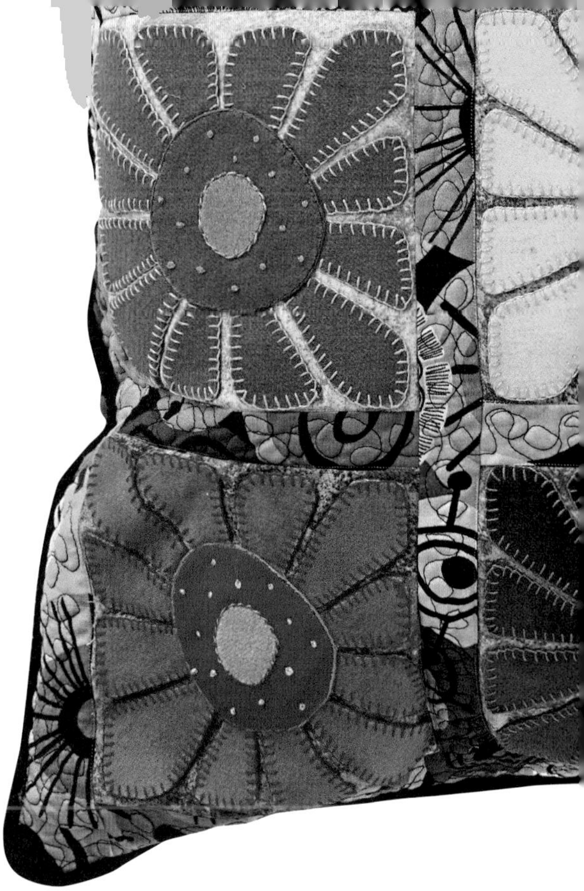

FINISHING

PIPING

1. Pin the flat edge of the piping to the edge of the pillow front, starting at the middle of the bottom and leaving a 1½″ end of the piping free. Pin all around, clipping at the corners. Using a zipper foot, machine baste all around, close to the cord.

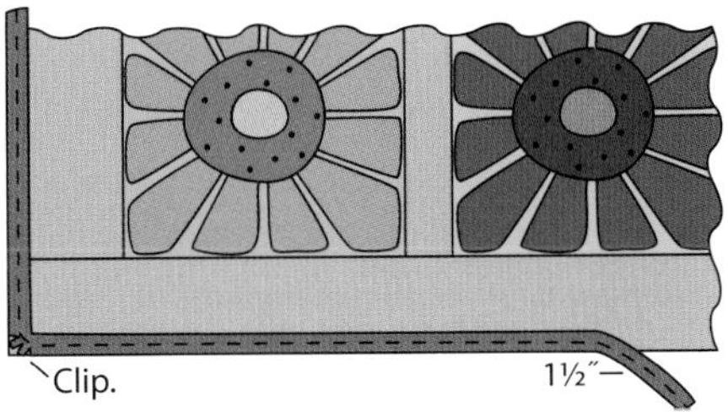

Baste piping.

2. When you reach the starting point, hold the free ends of the piping together and let them curve off the pillow's edge. Stitch down. Trim the piping ends even with the seam allowance.

PILLOW BACK

1. Fold under ¼″ along one long edge of each pillow back rectangle and press. Fold under another ¼″ and press again. Topstitch in place.

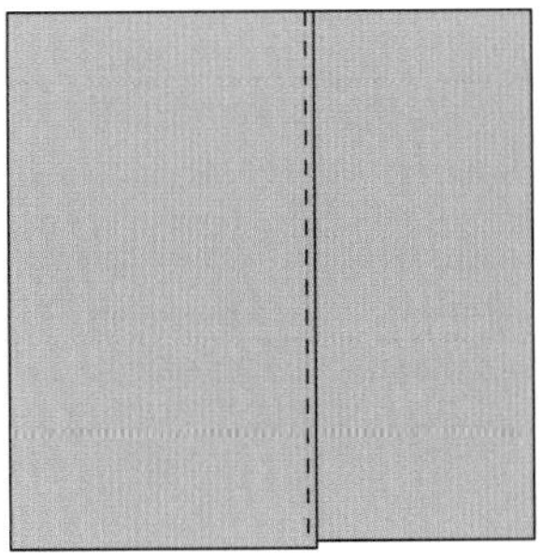

Pillow back

2. Overlap the hemmed edges so the back measures 24½″ × 24½″.

3. Place the pillow front right side up. With right sides together, place the pillow back pieces on the front, with the raw edges matching and the hemmed edges overlapping in the middle. Using a zipper foot, sew on the basting line around the outside edges.

4. Trim the corners and turn the pillow cover right side out. Place the pillow form inside the pillow cover through the opening in the back.

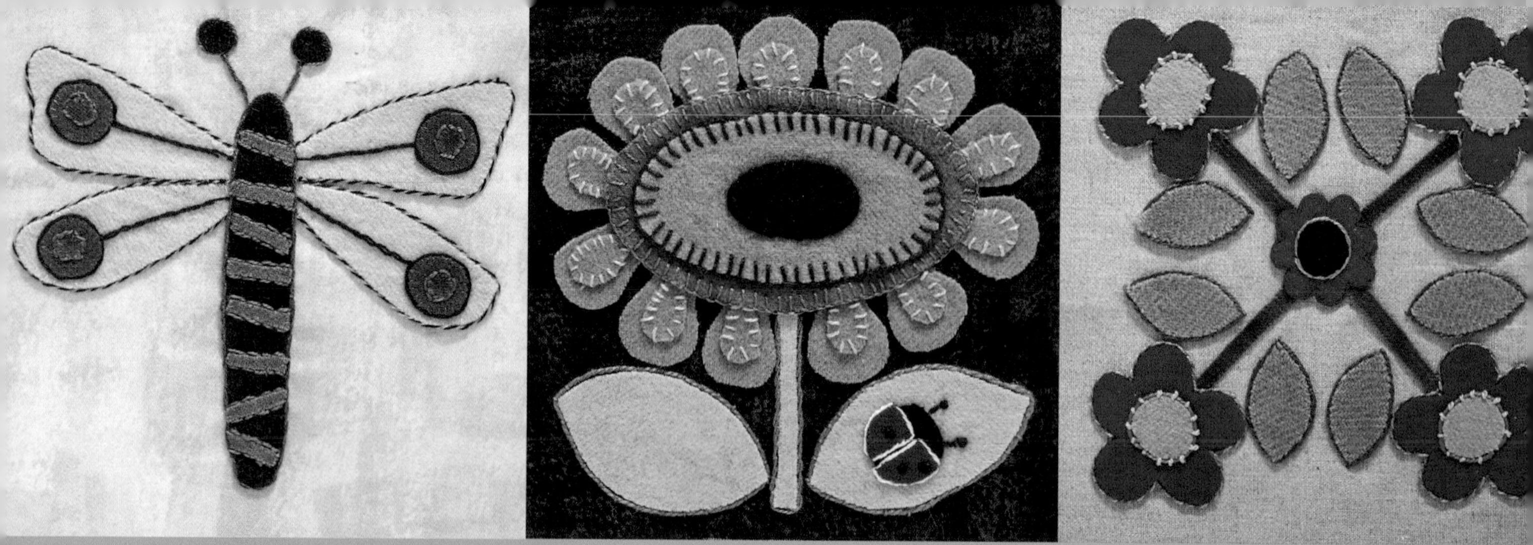

The Blocks

1
2
3
4
5
6
7
8
6R
7R
8R

6
6R
1
2
3
4
5
8
7
8R
7R

1
2
3
4
5
6
7
7R
6R

MORNING GLORY
Block D

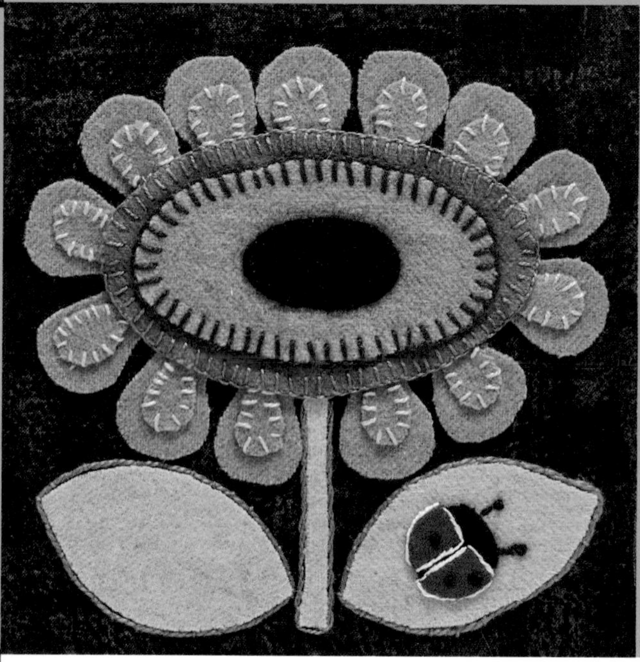

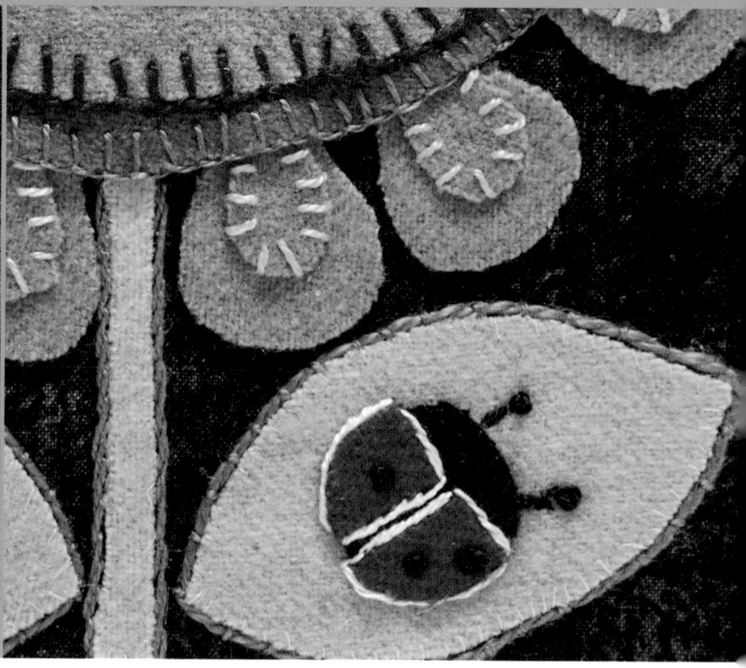

Garden Whimsy

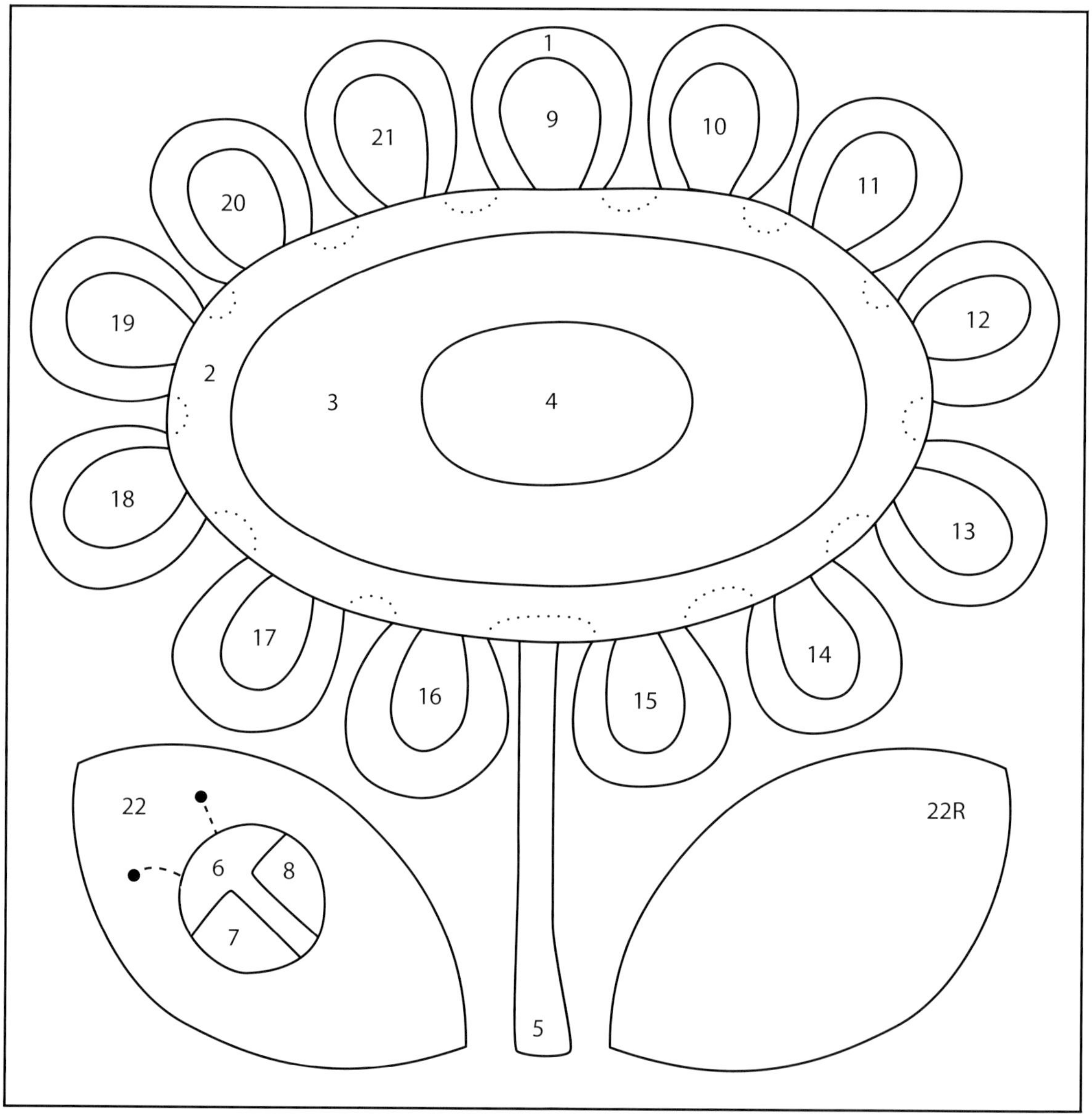

SPECKLED BUBBLE FLOWER
Block E

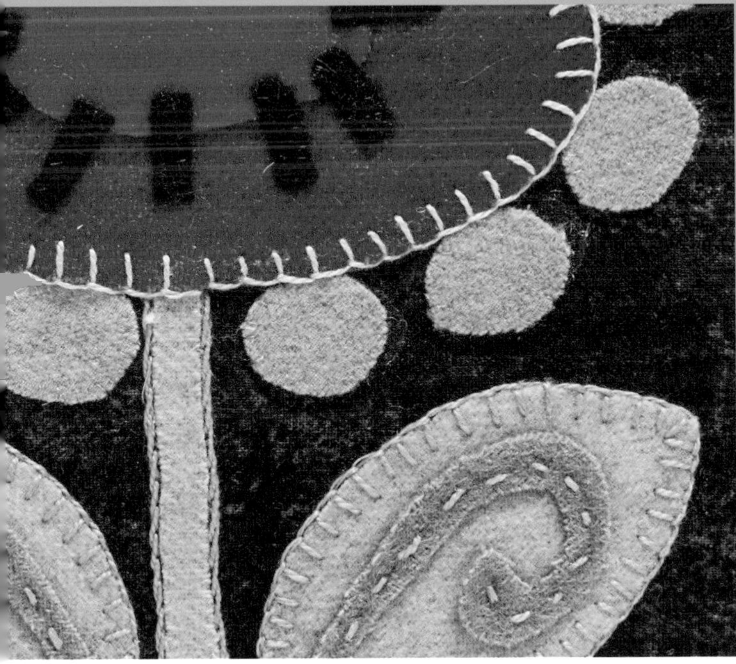

SUNDANCE
Block F

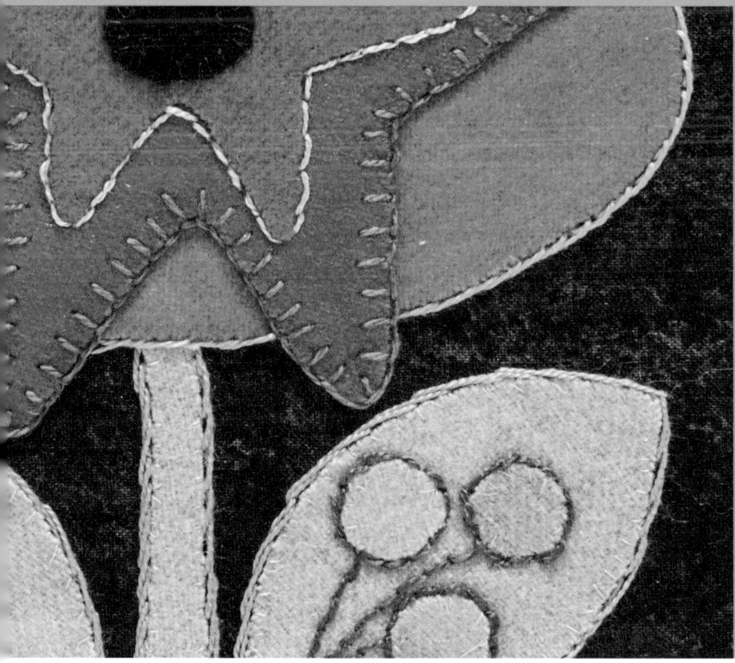

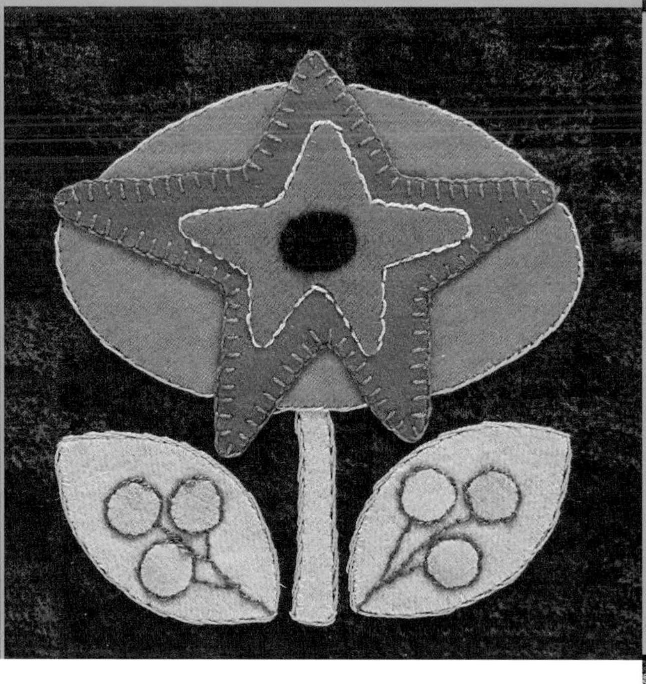

STAR FLOWER
Block G

LAZY DAISY
Block H

Garden Whimsy

FRINGED HAPPY FLOWER

Block 1

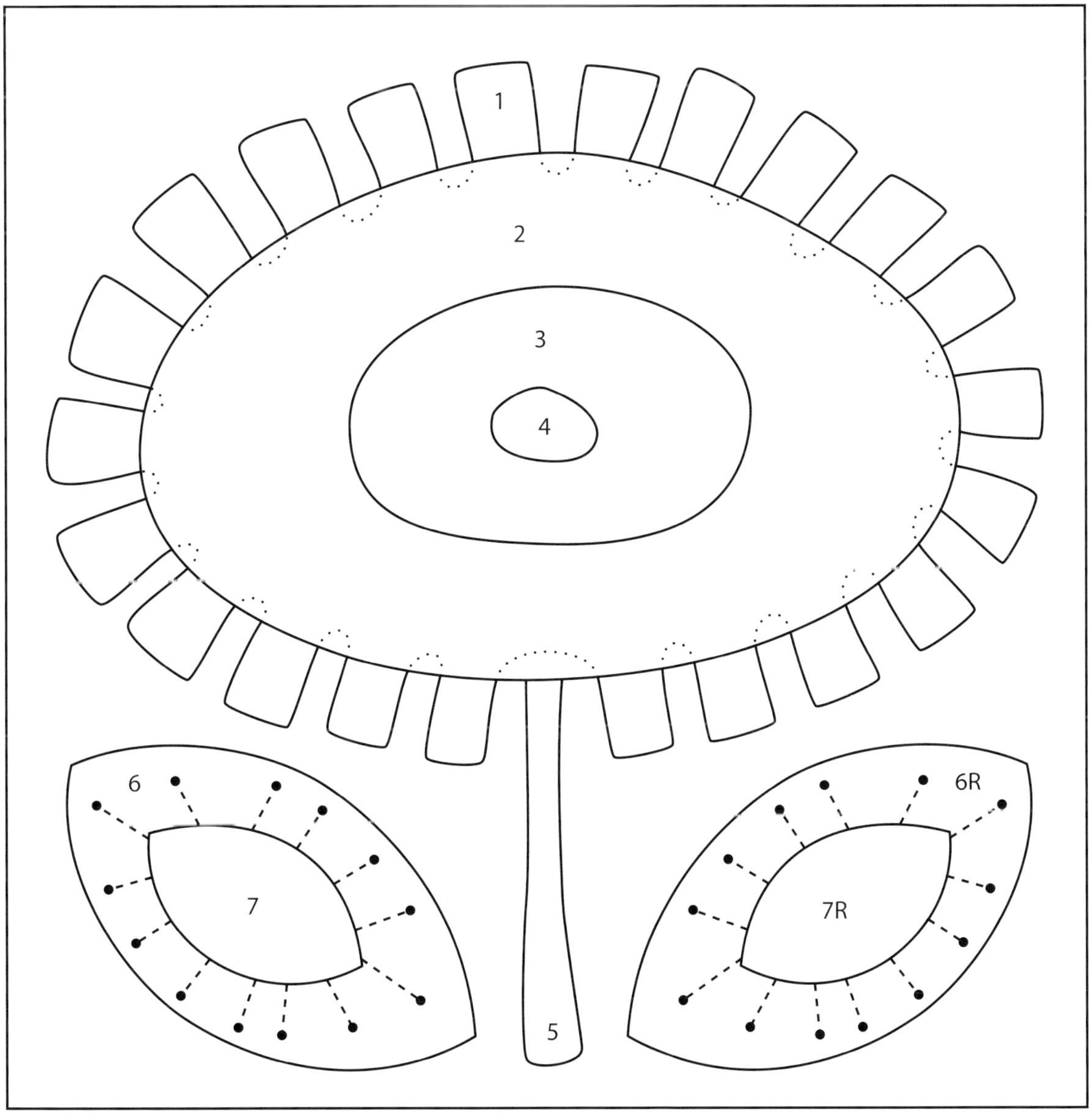

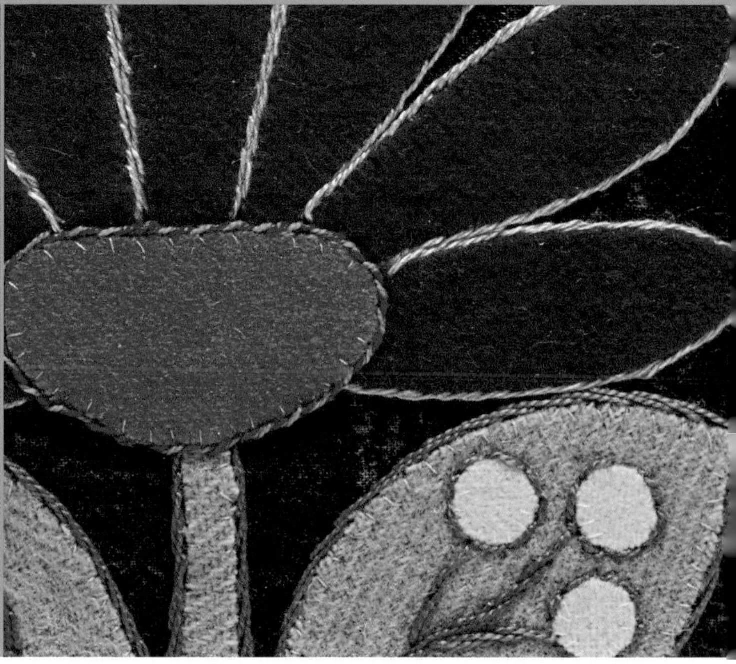

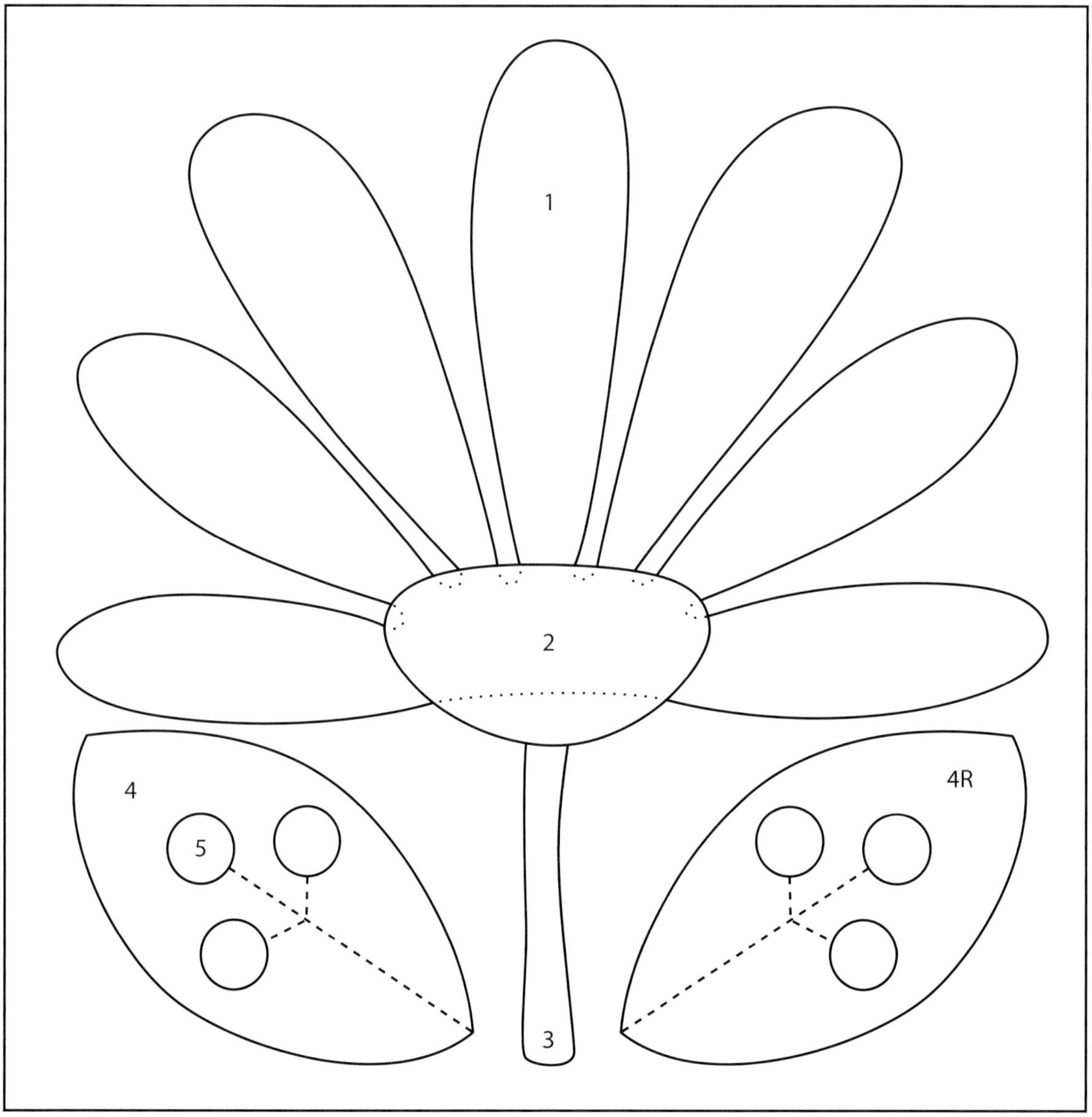
1
2
3
4
5
4R

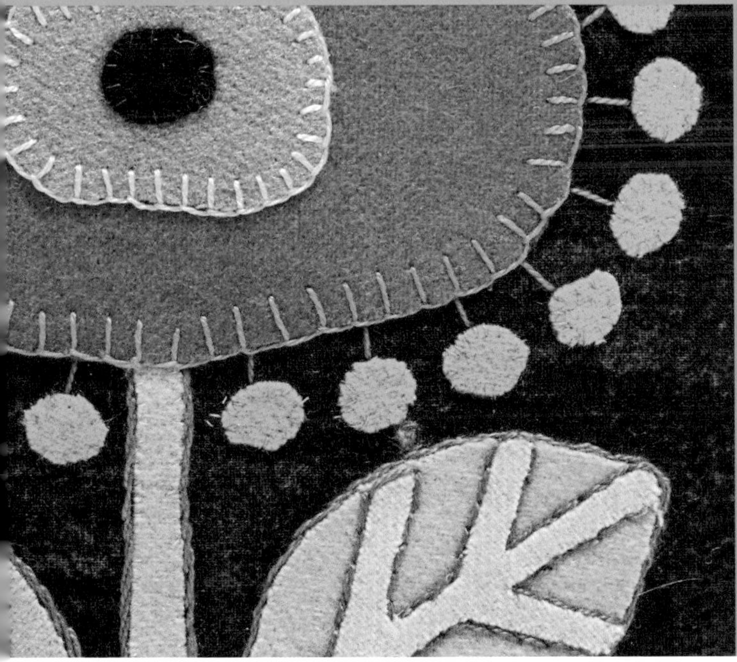

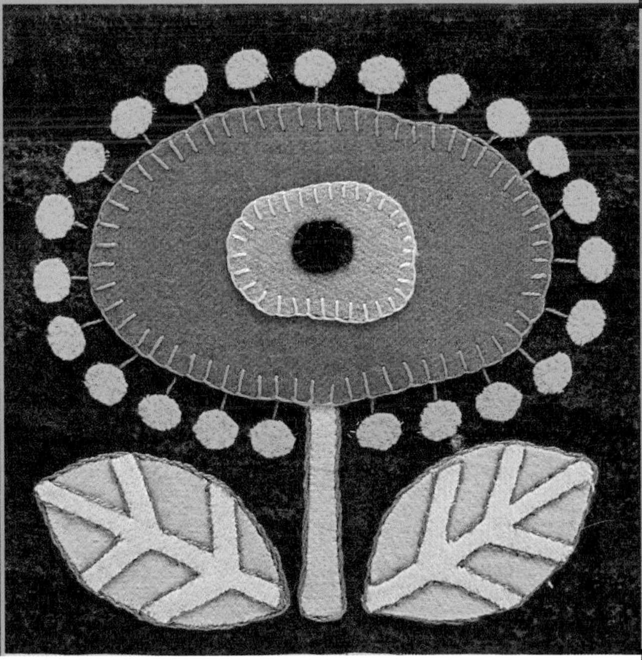

BALL FLOWER

Block K

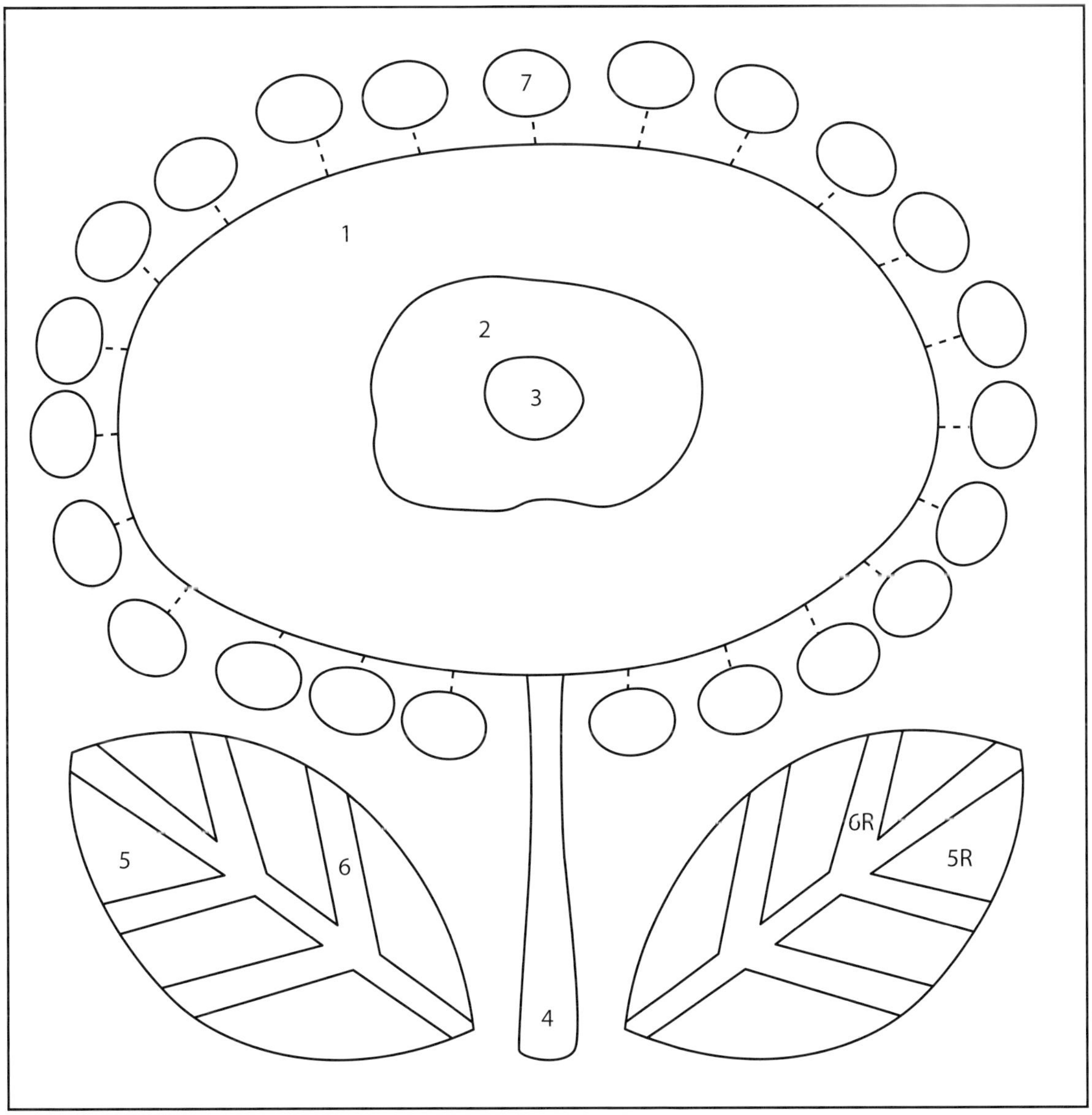

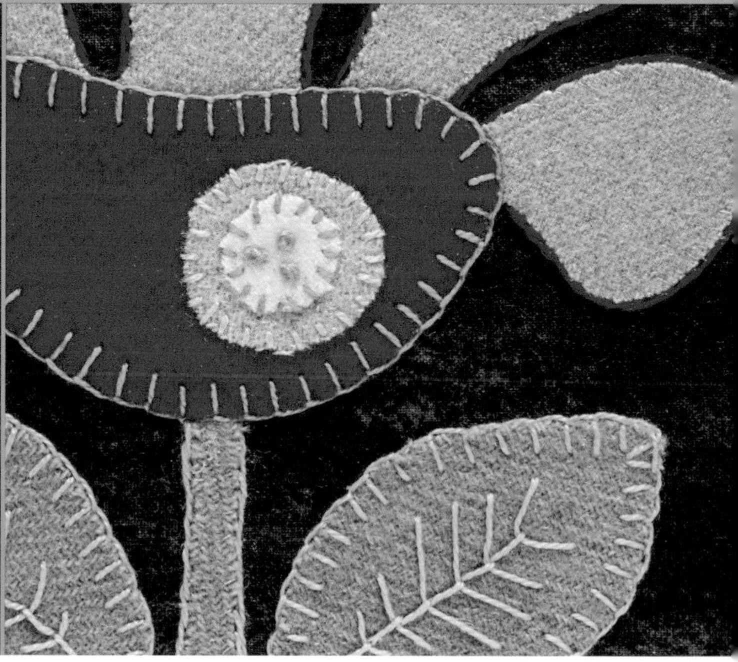

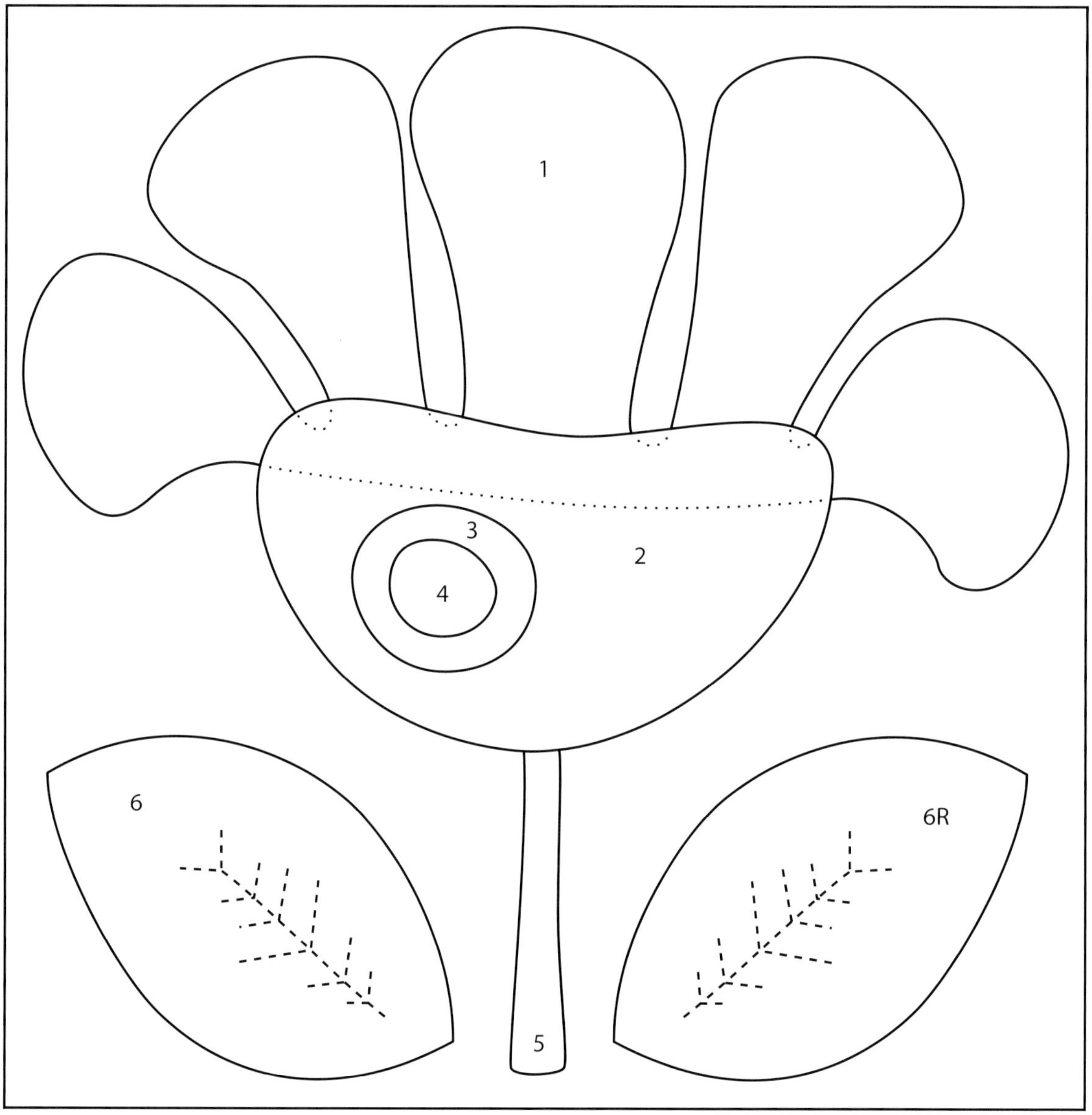
1
2
3
4
5
6
6R

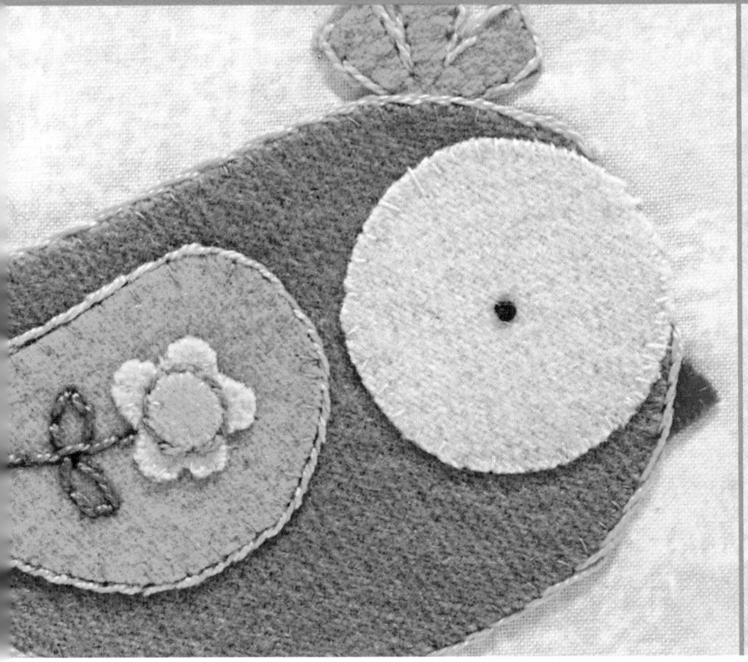

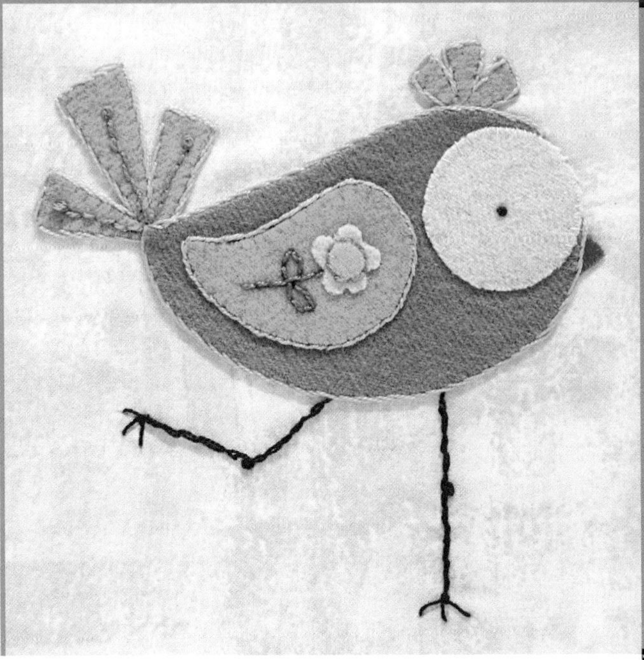

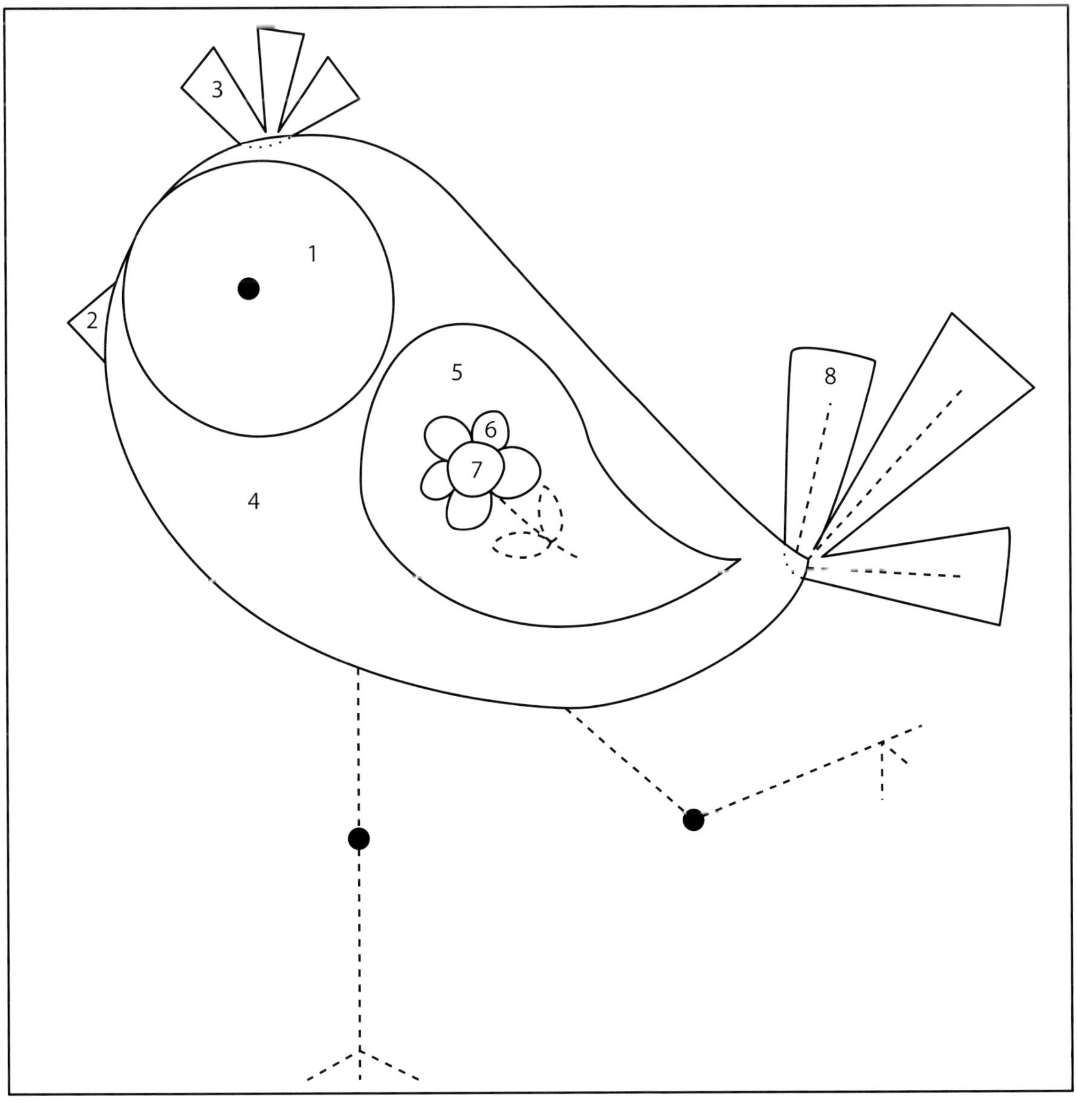
1
2
3
4
5
6
7
8

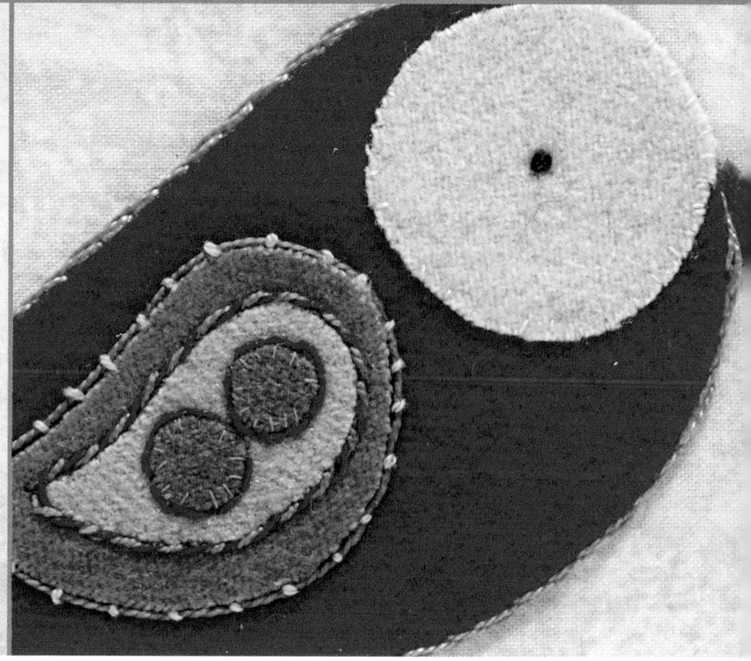

1
2
4
6
5
7
3
8

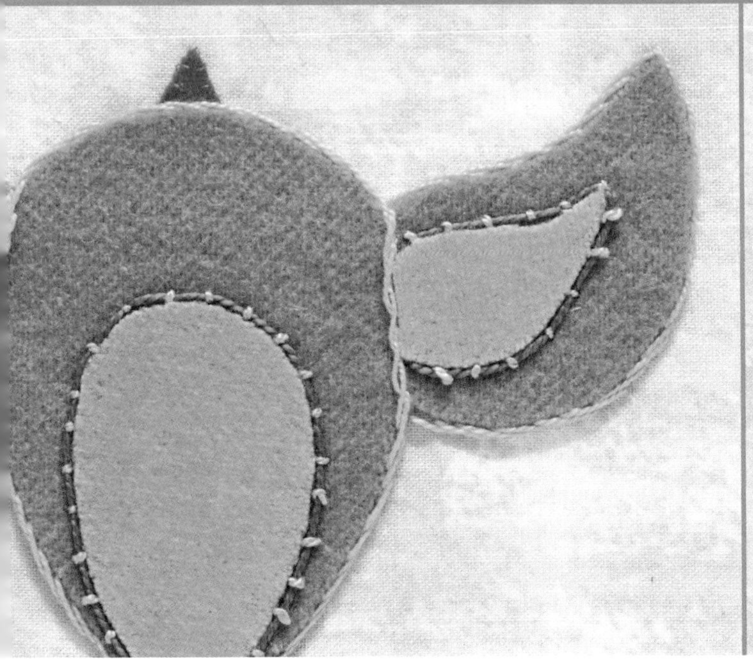

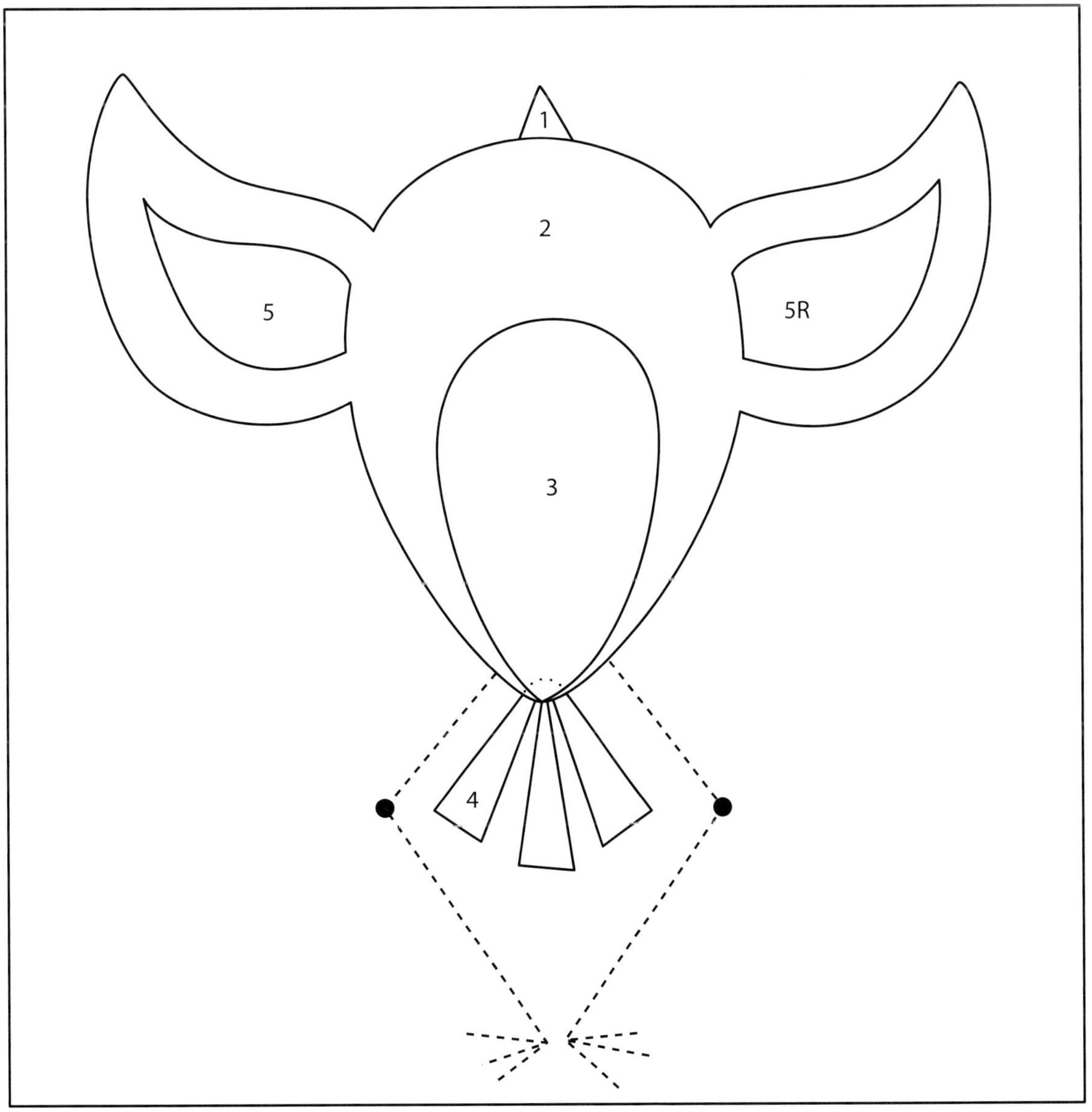
1
2
5
5R
3
4

1
2
3
4
5
6
7

PURPLE BIRD
Block E

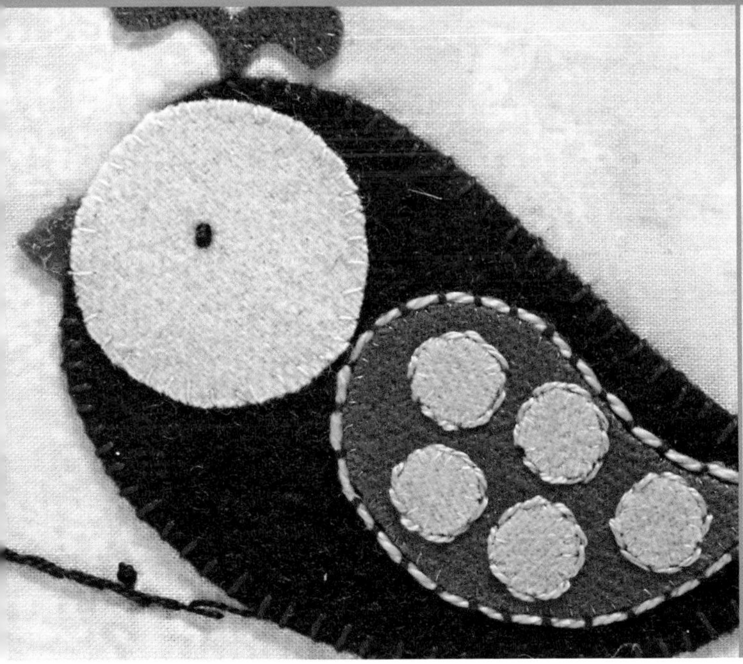

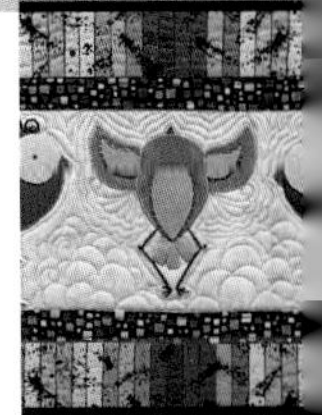

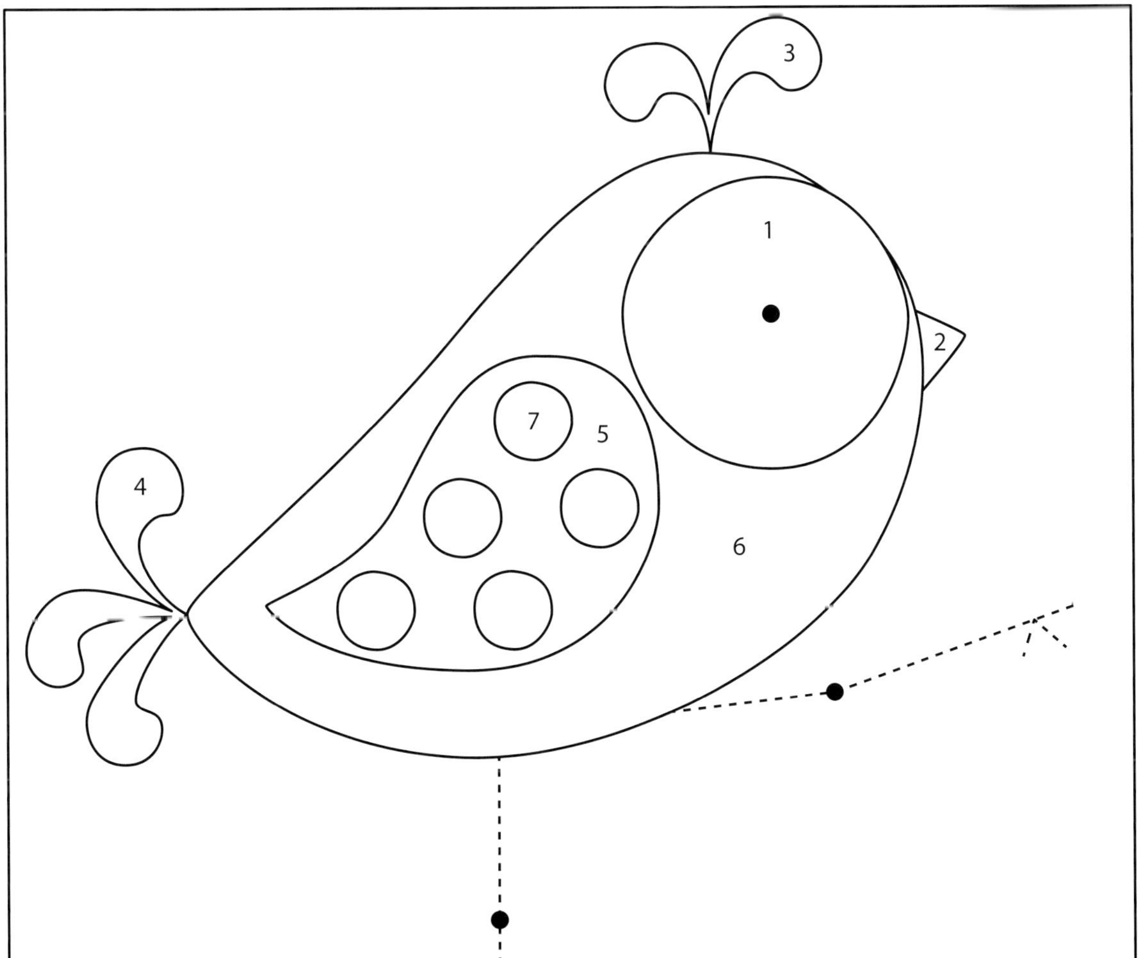

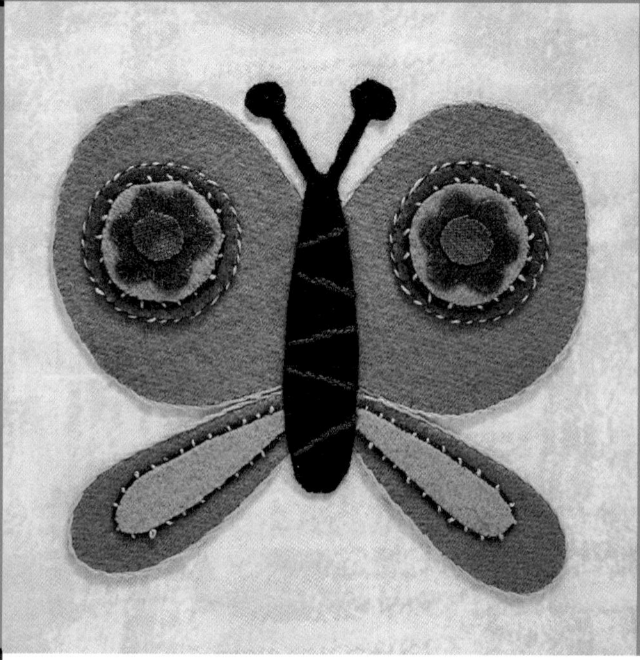

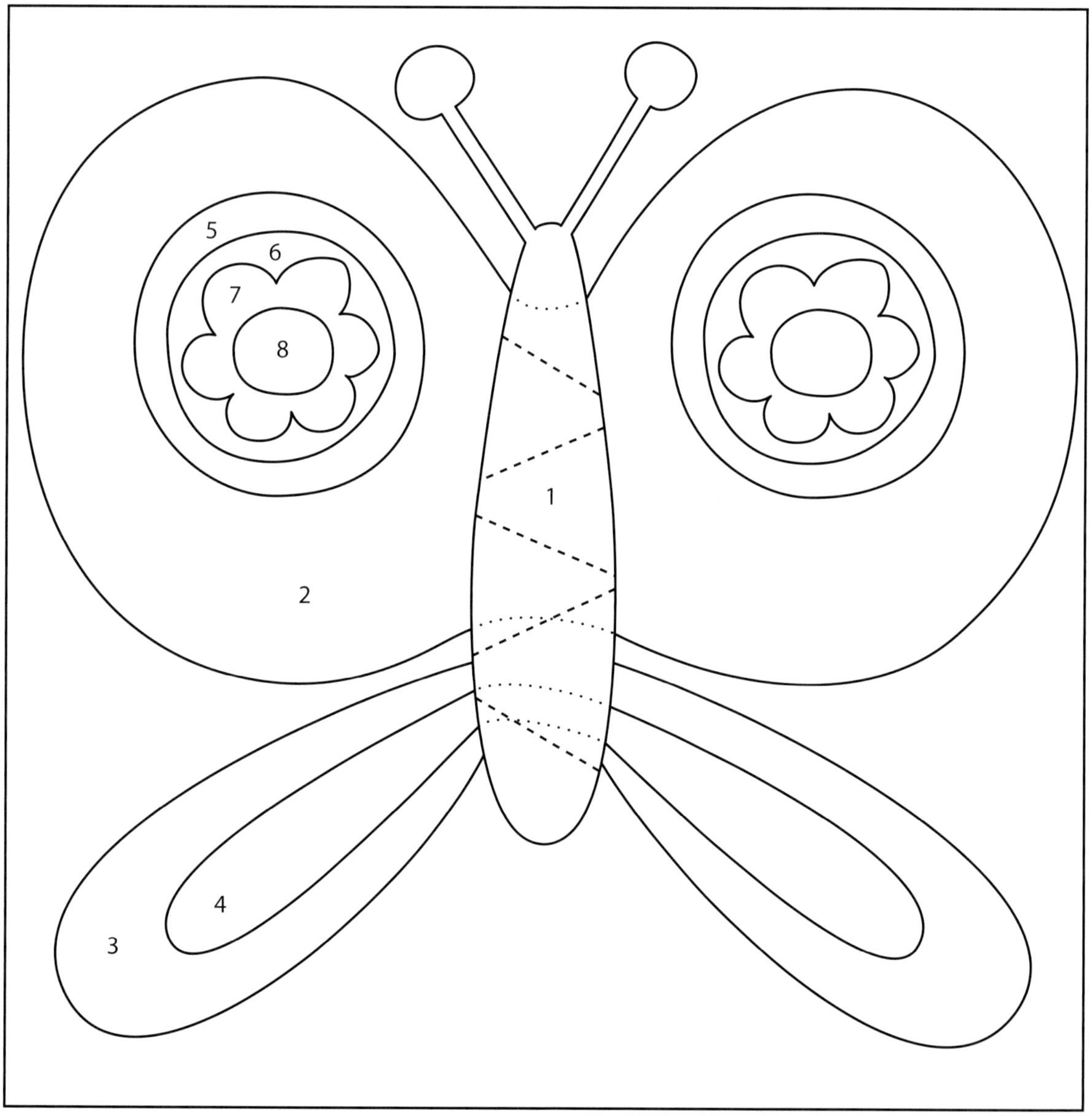
1
2
3
4
5
6
7
8

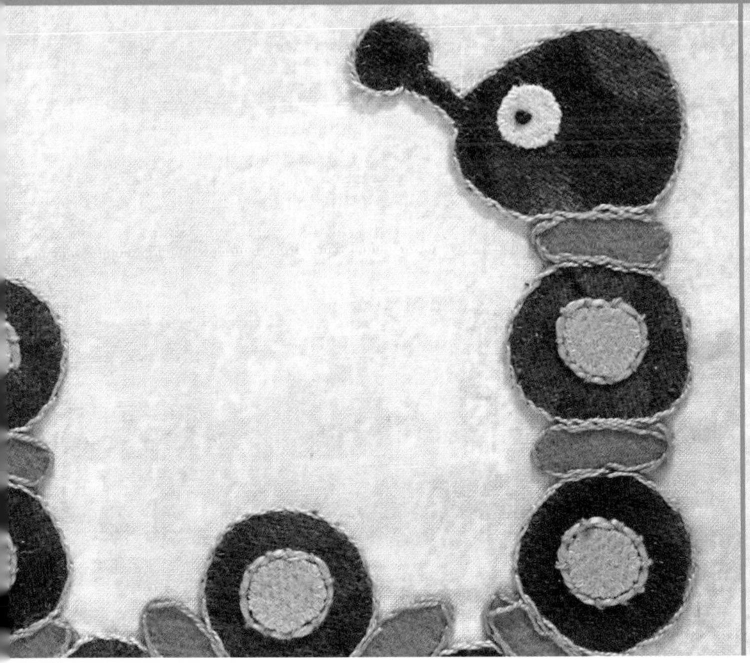

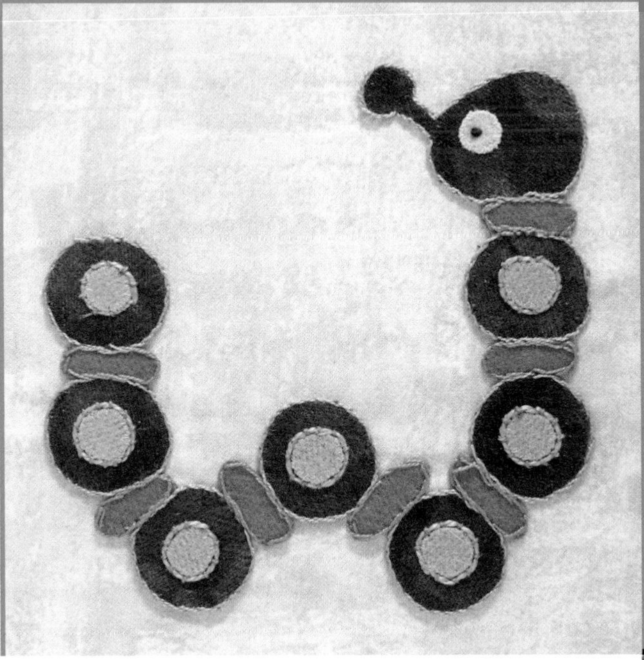

CATERPILLAR

Block B

5
4
2
1
3

BUMBLEBEE
Block D

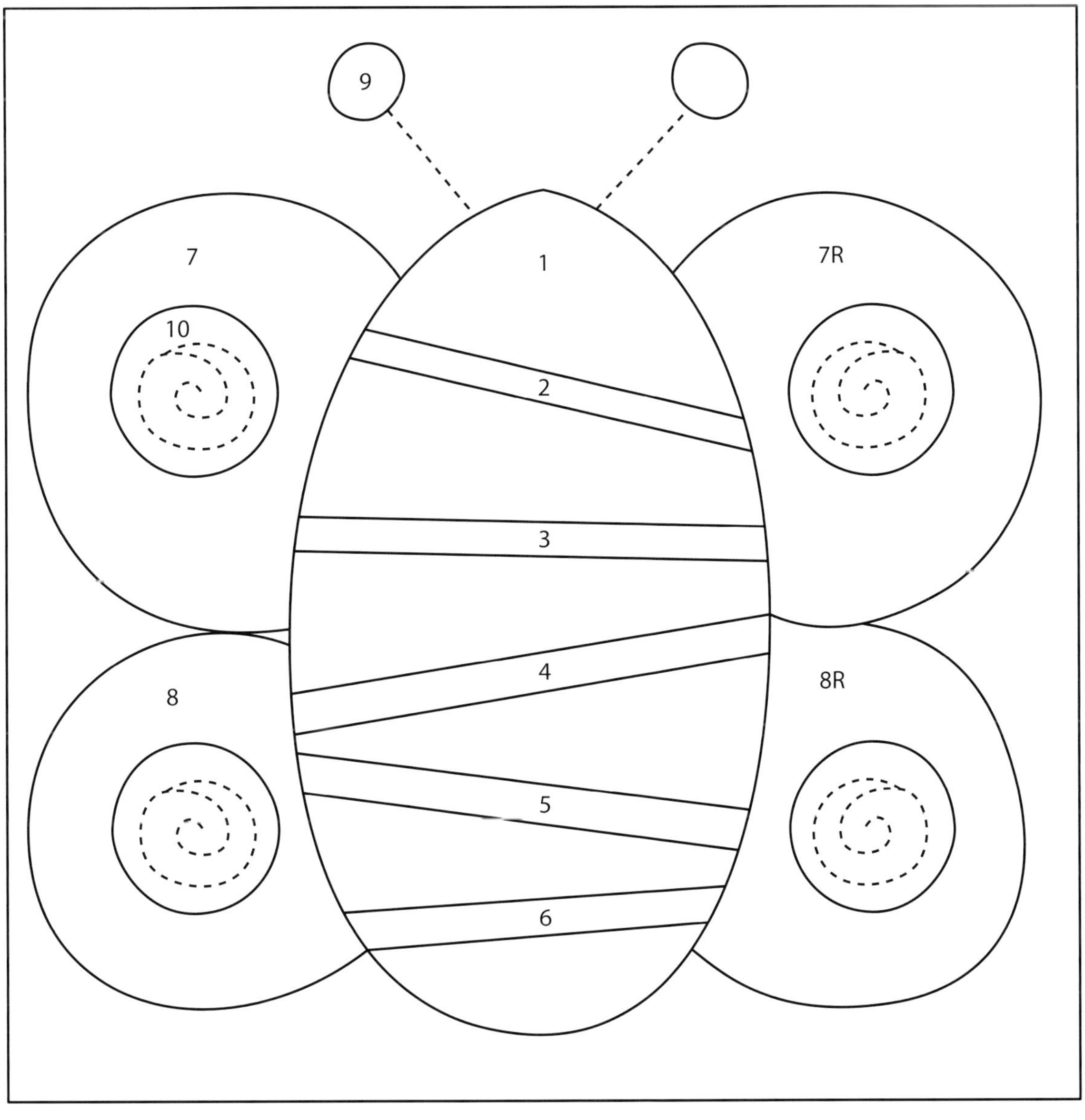

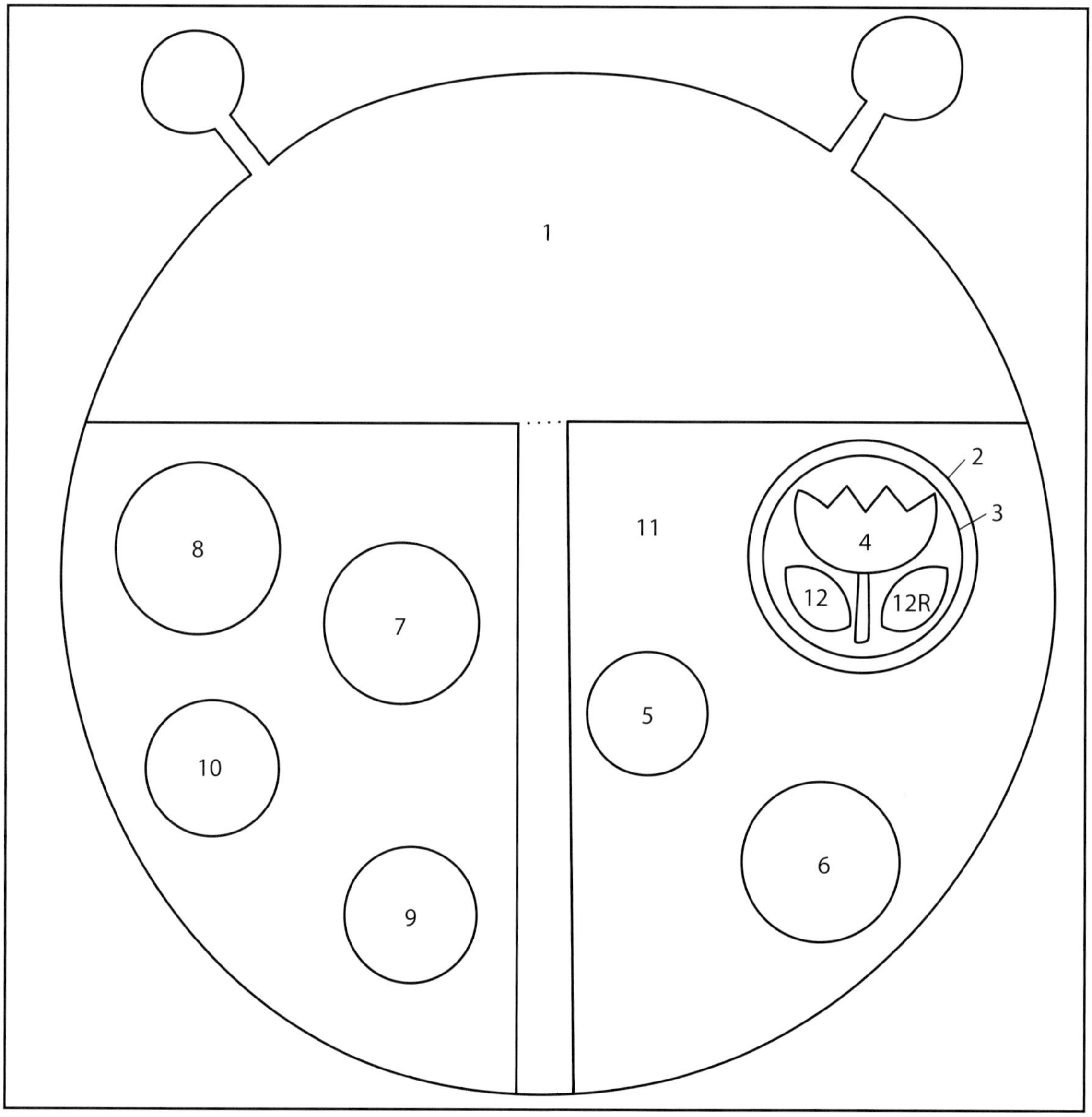
1
2
3
4
11
12
12R
8
7
5
10
6
9

DRAGONFLY
Block F

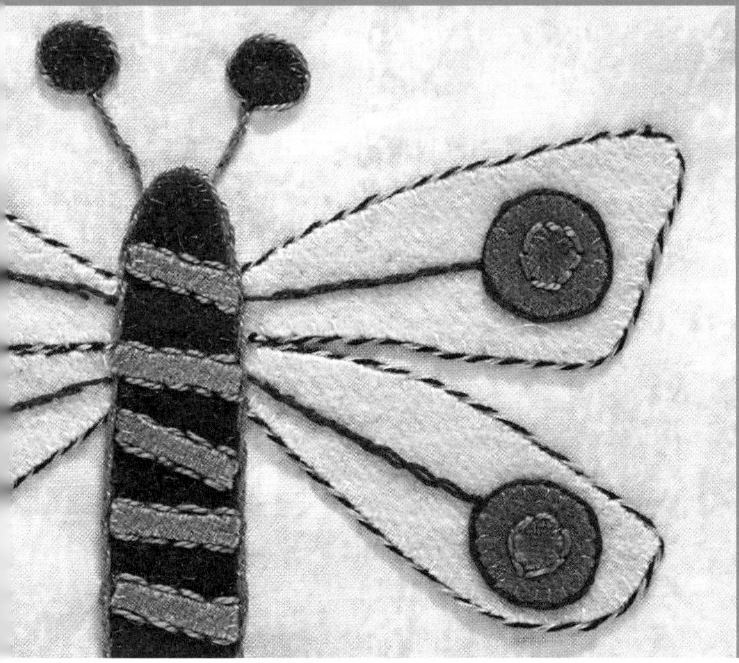

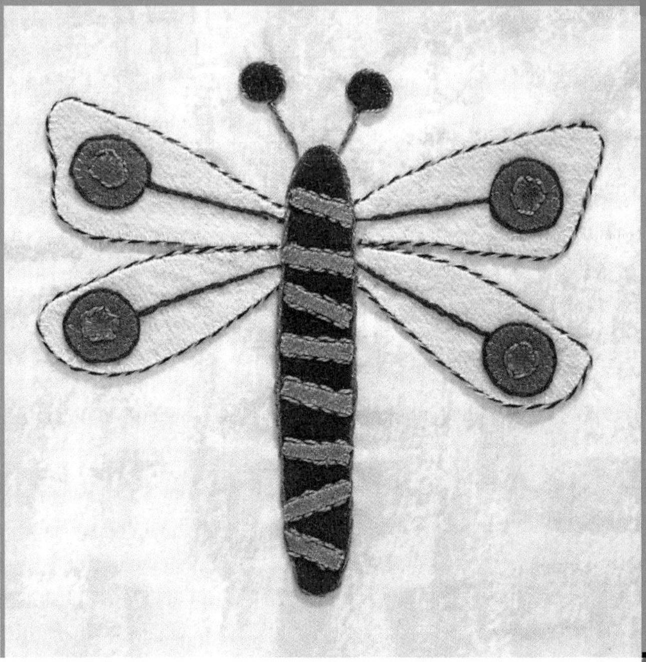

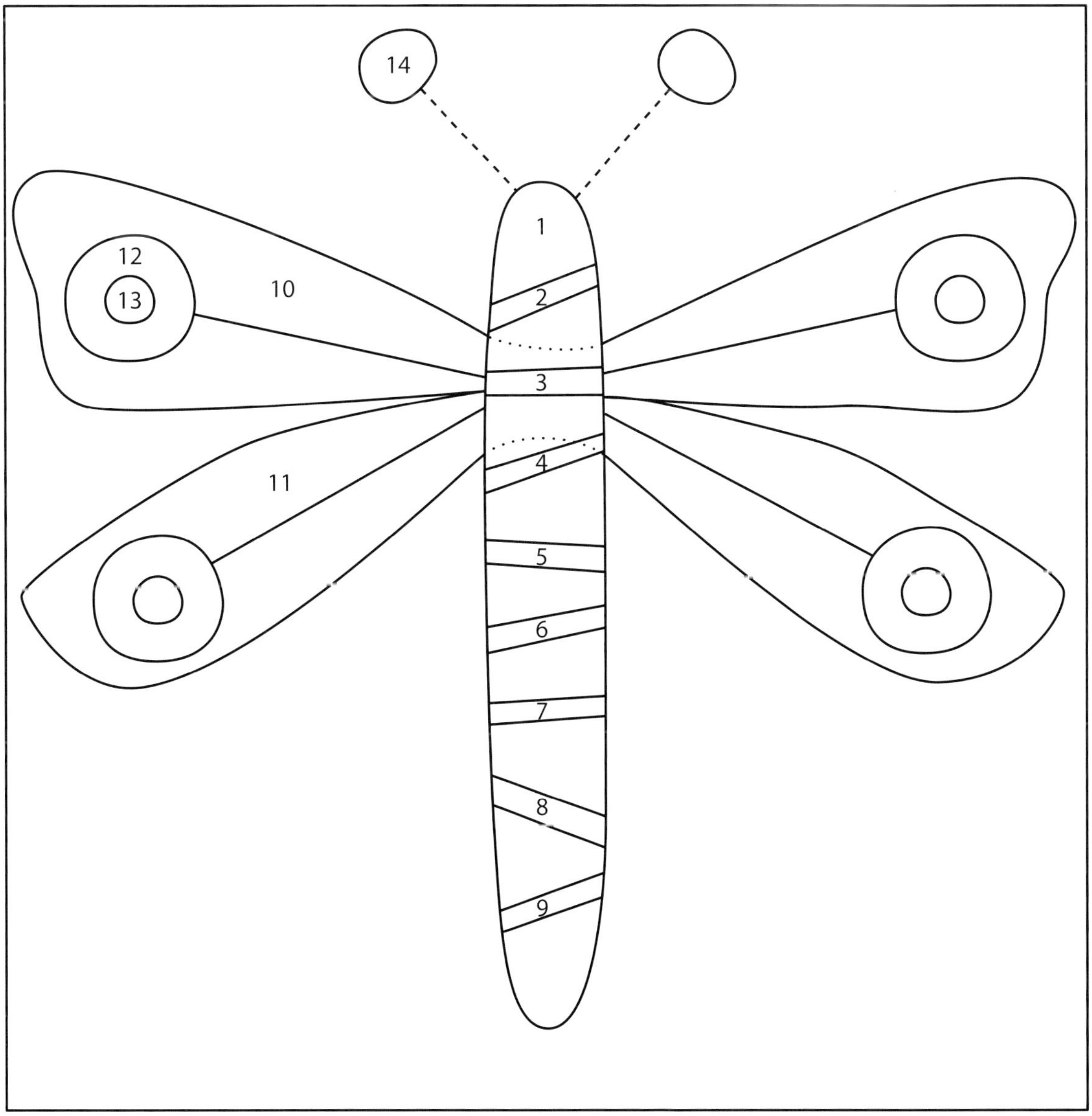

1
2
3
4

1
2
4
3

DAZZLE FLOWER
Block C

1
2
3

1
3
2

WILDFLOWER
Block F

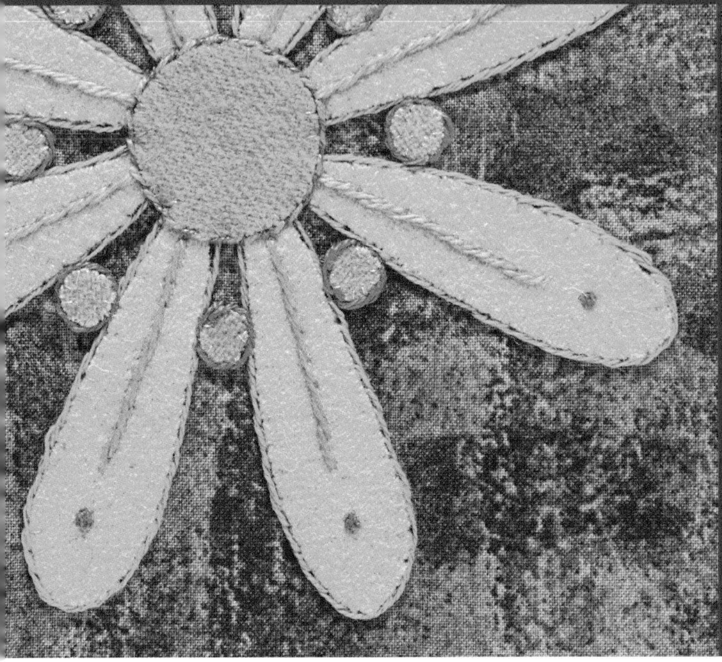

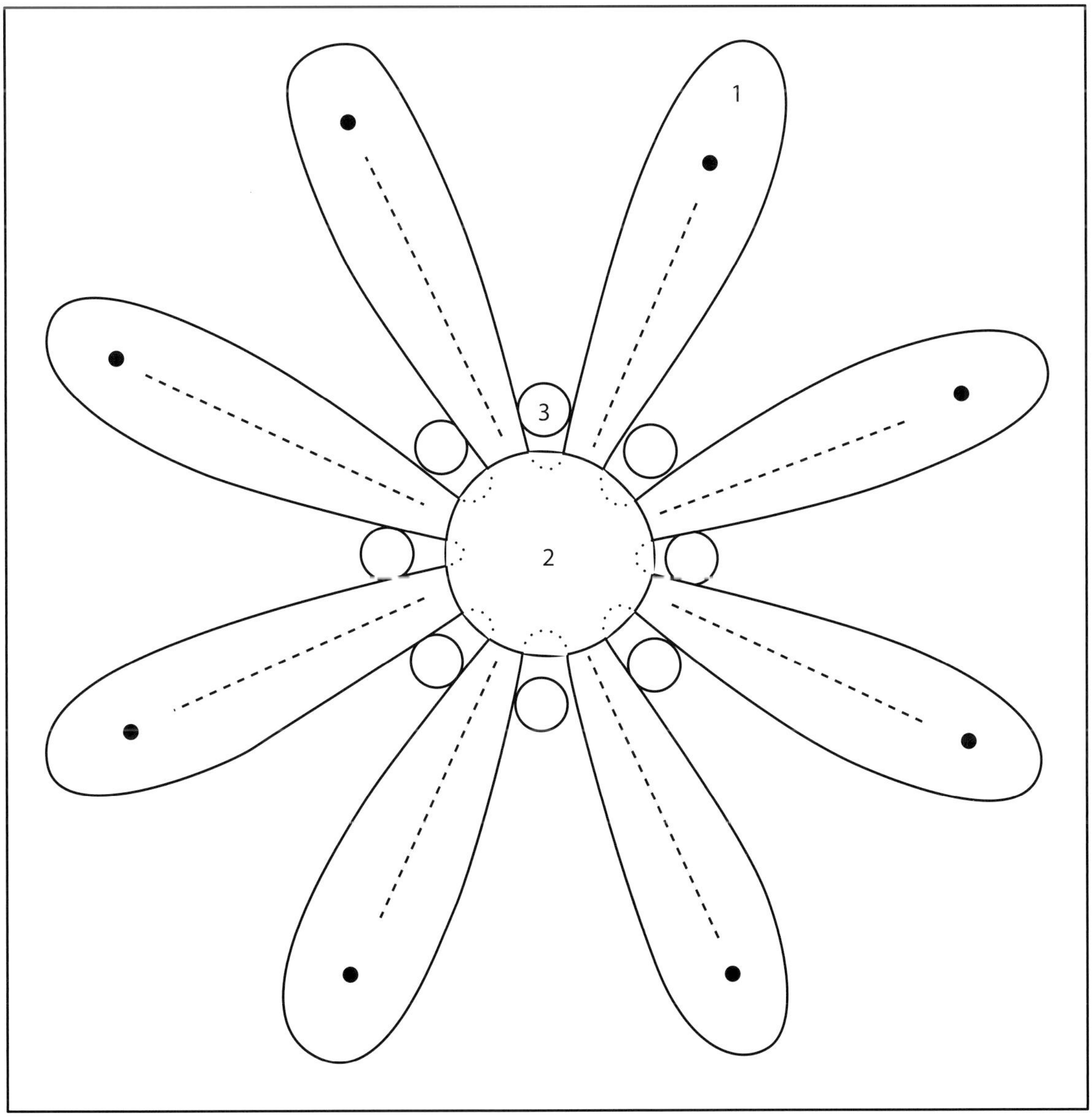

CORNER SQUARE & LEAVES

Bloomin' Beauties

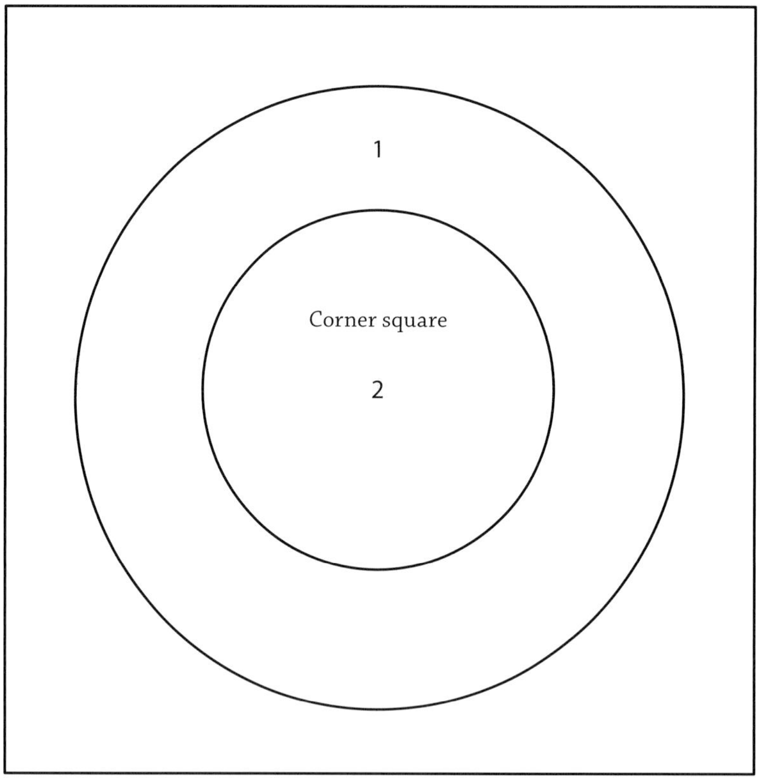

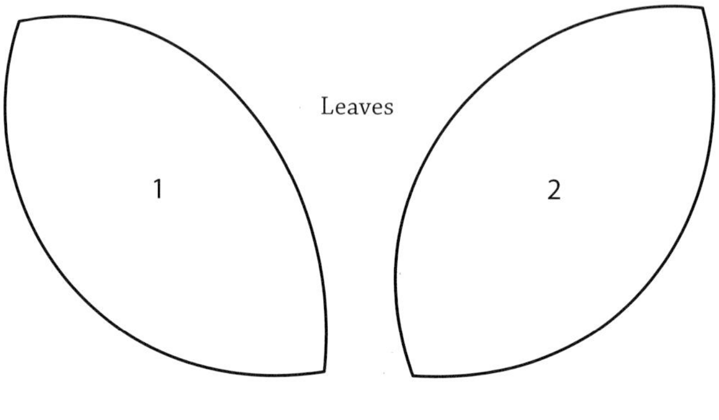

1
2
3
4
5

3
4
5
6
2
1

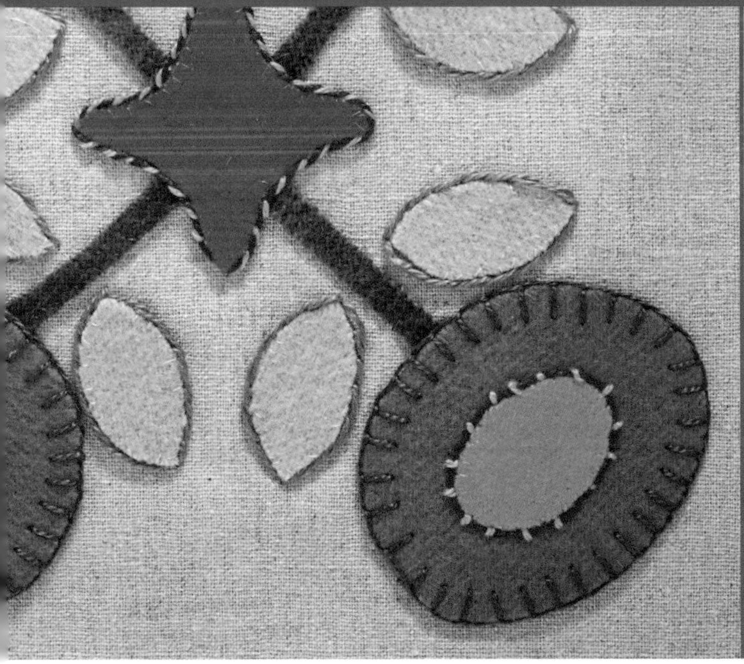

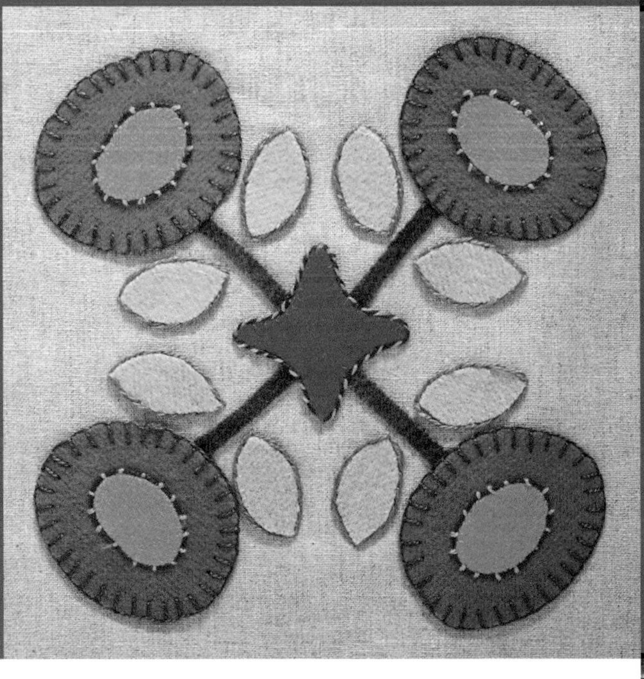

DIZZY IZZI
Block C

3
4
5
2
6
1

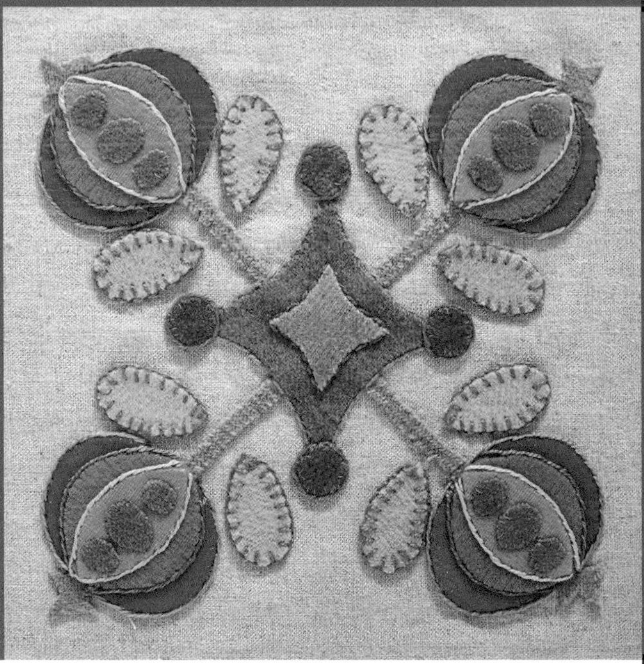

4
5
6
7
8
9
3
10
2
11
1

LUCI LU
Block F

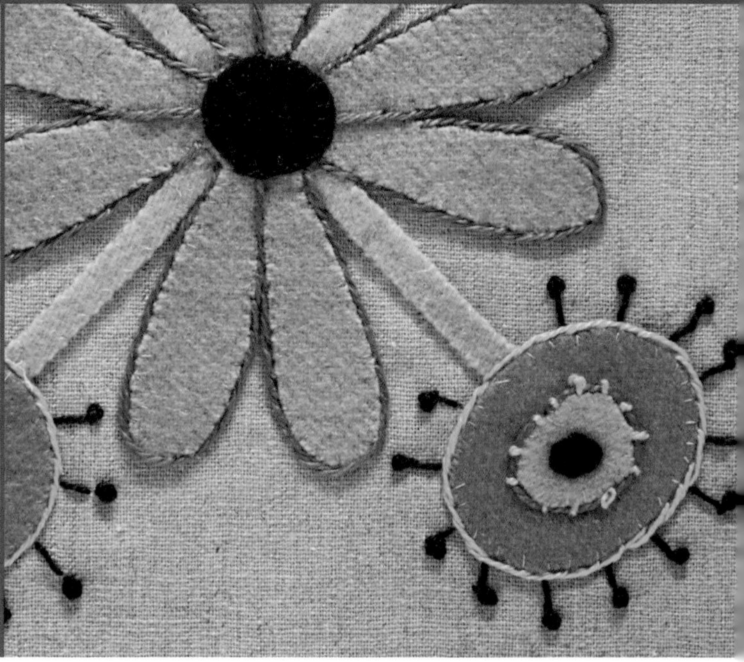

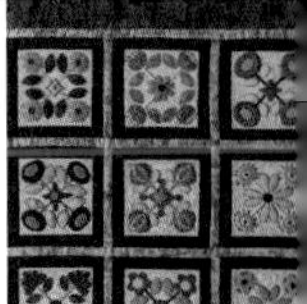

1
2
3
4

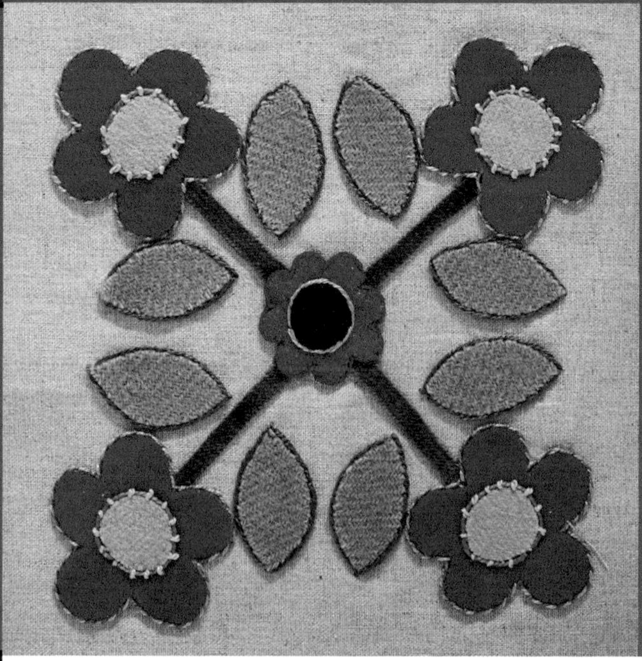

3
4
5
6
2
1

3
4
5
6
2
1

BLUEBELL
Block A

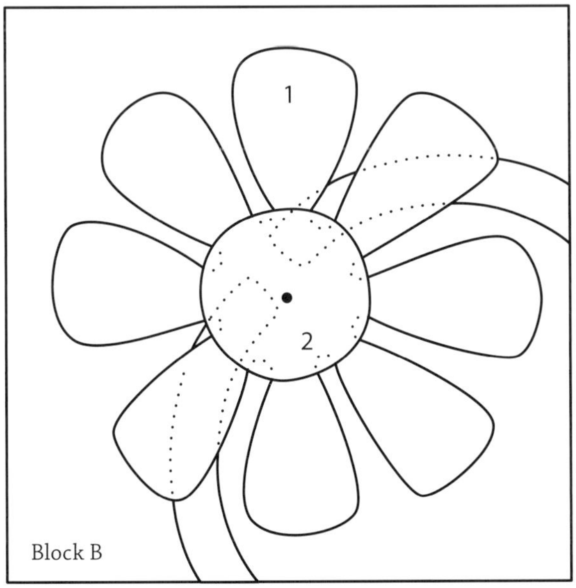
1
2
Block B

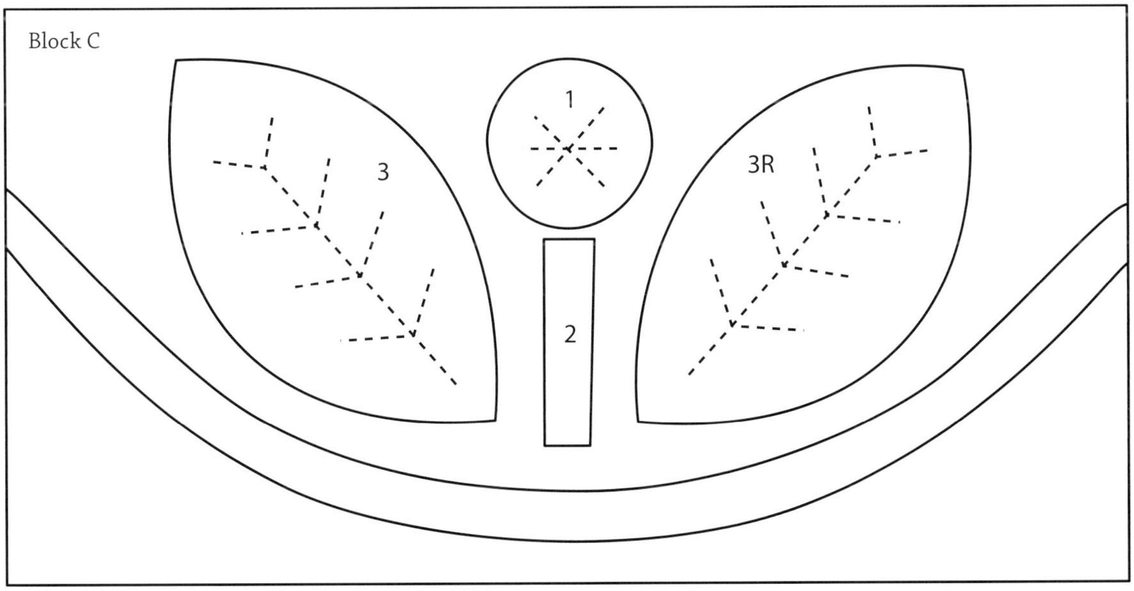
Block C
1
3
3R
2

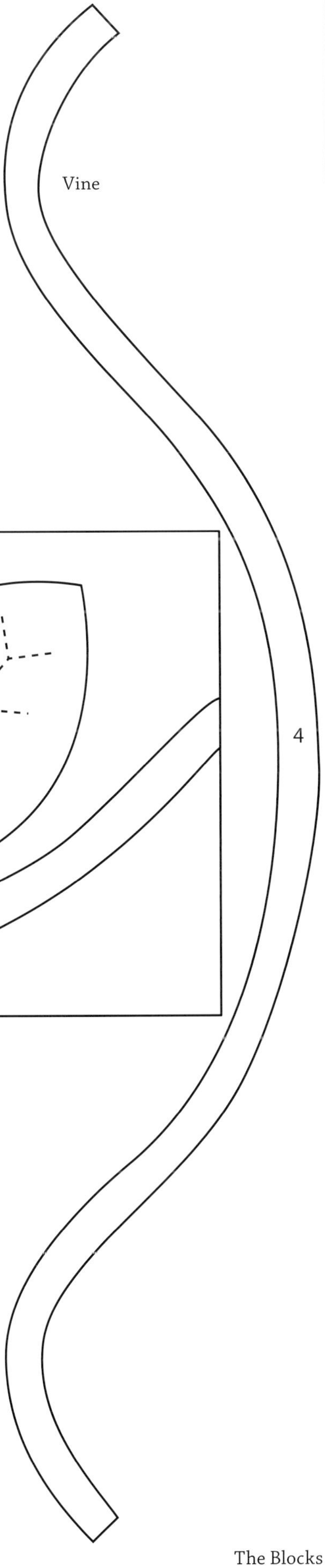
Vine
4

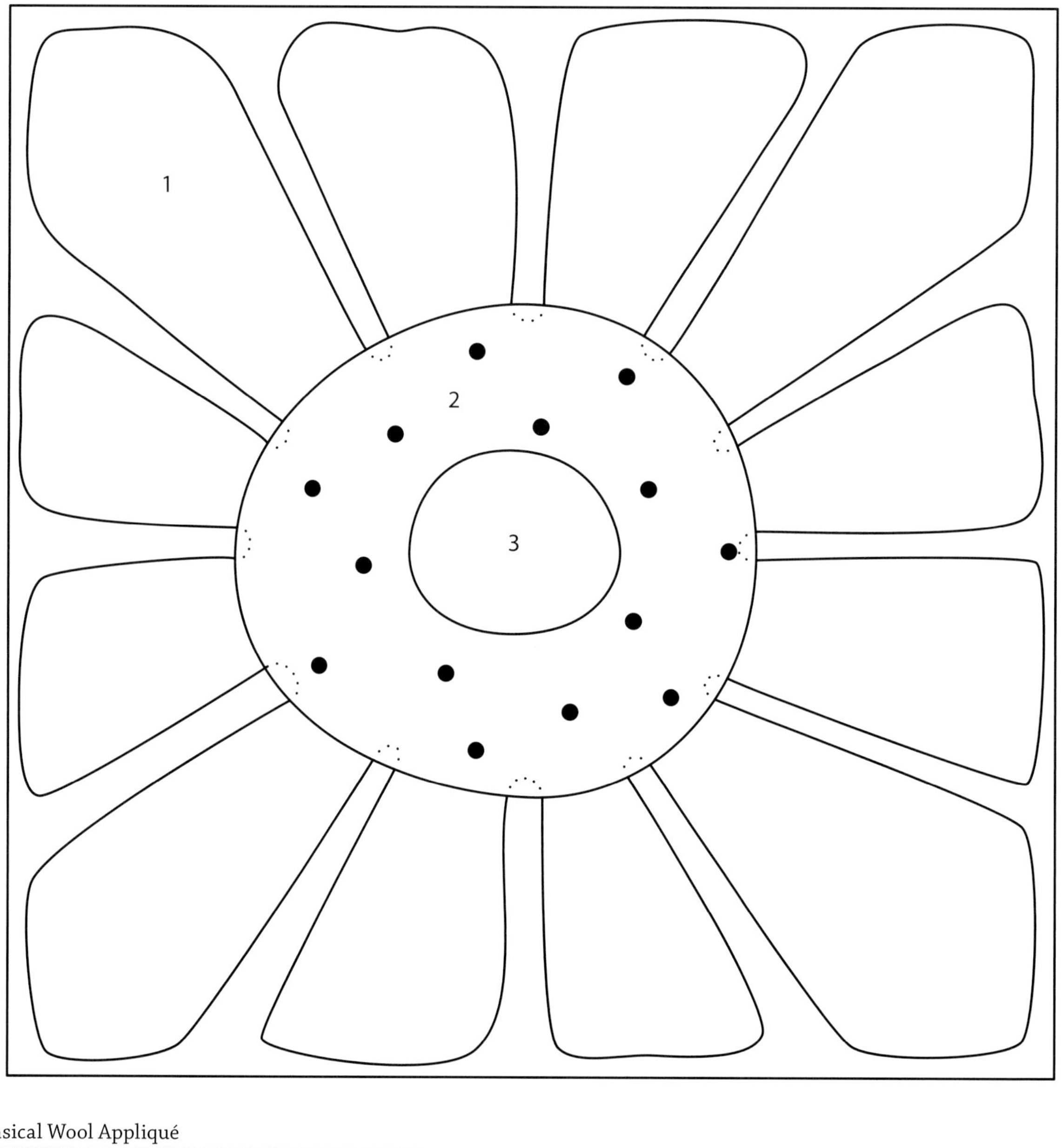
1
2
3

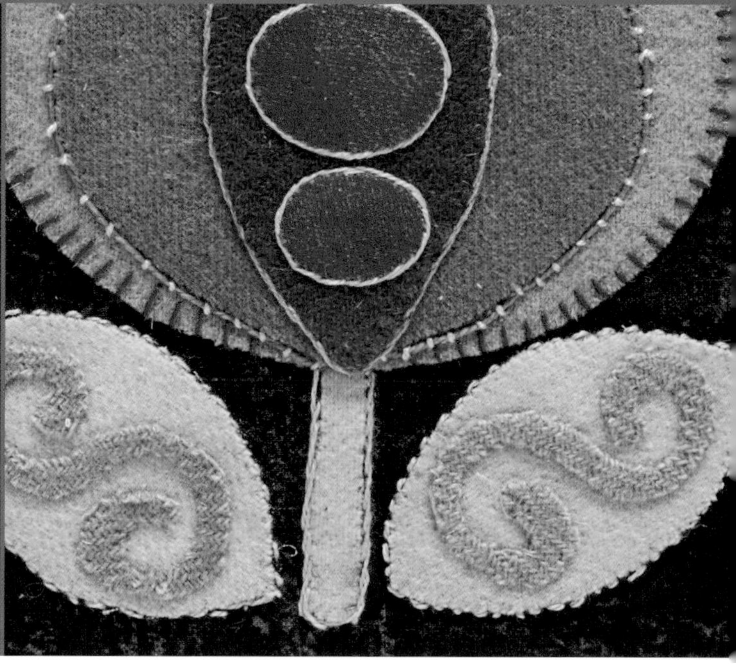

WALLFLOWER

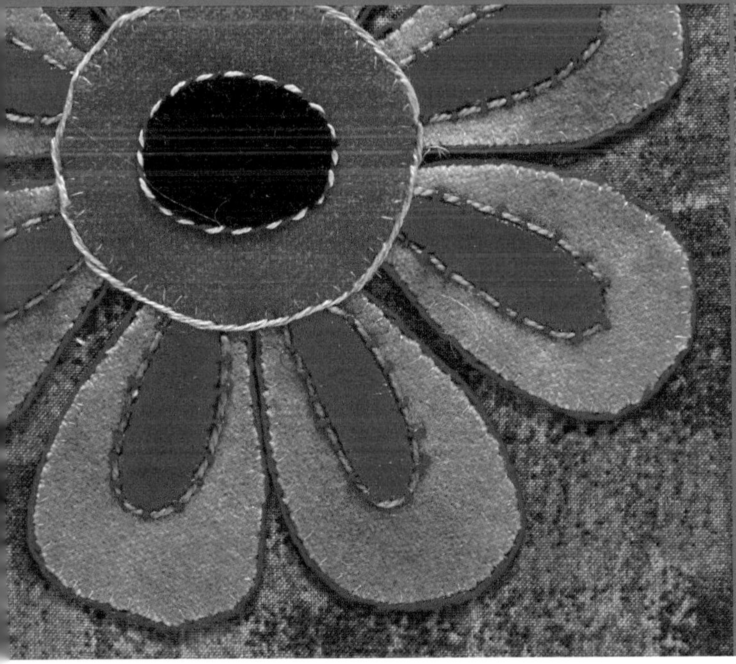

SUNFLOWER

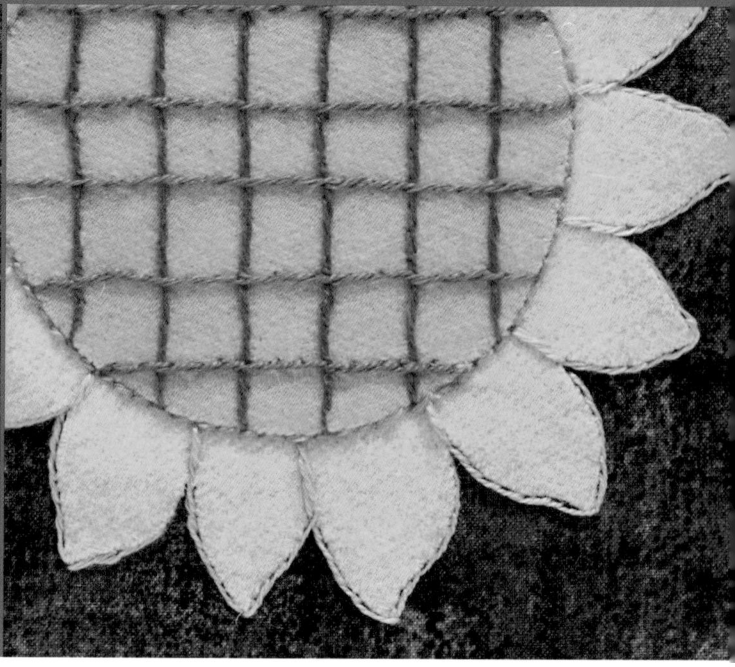

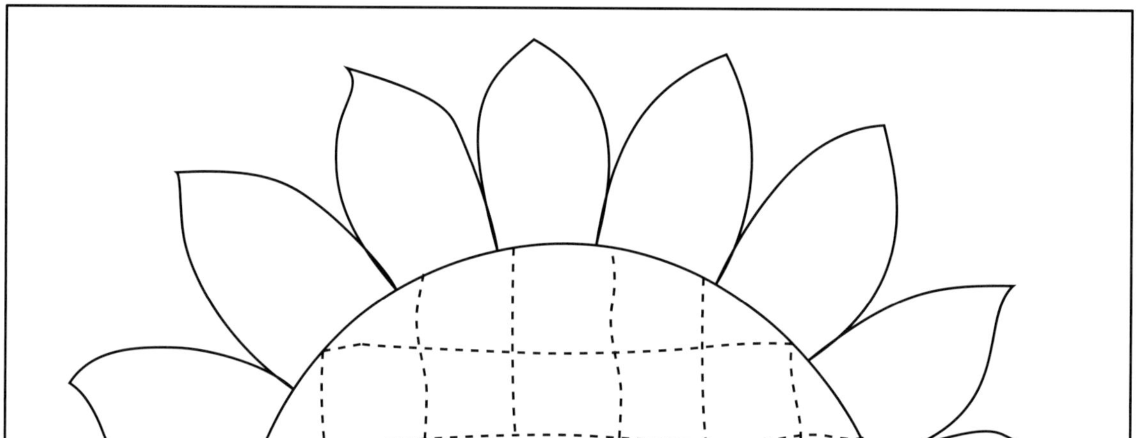

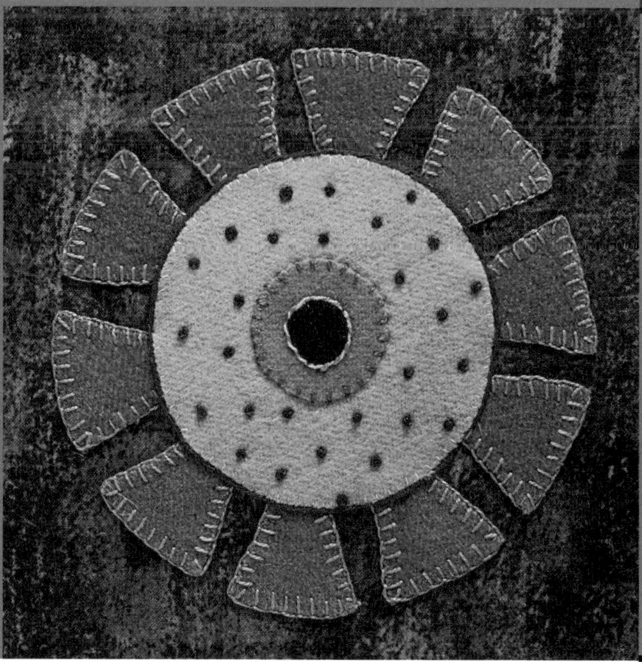

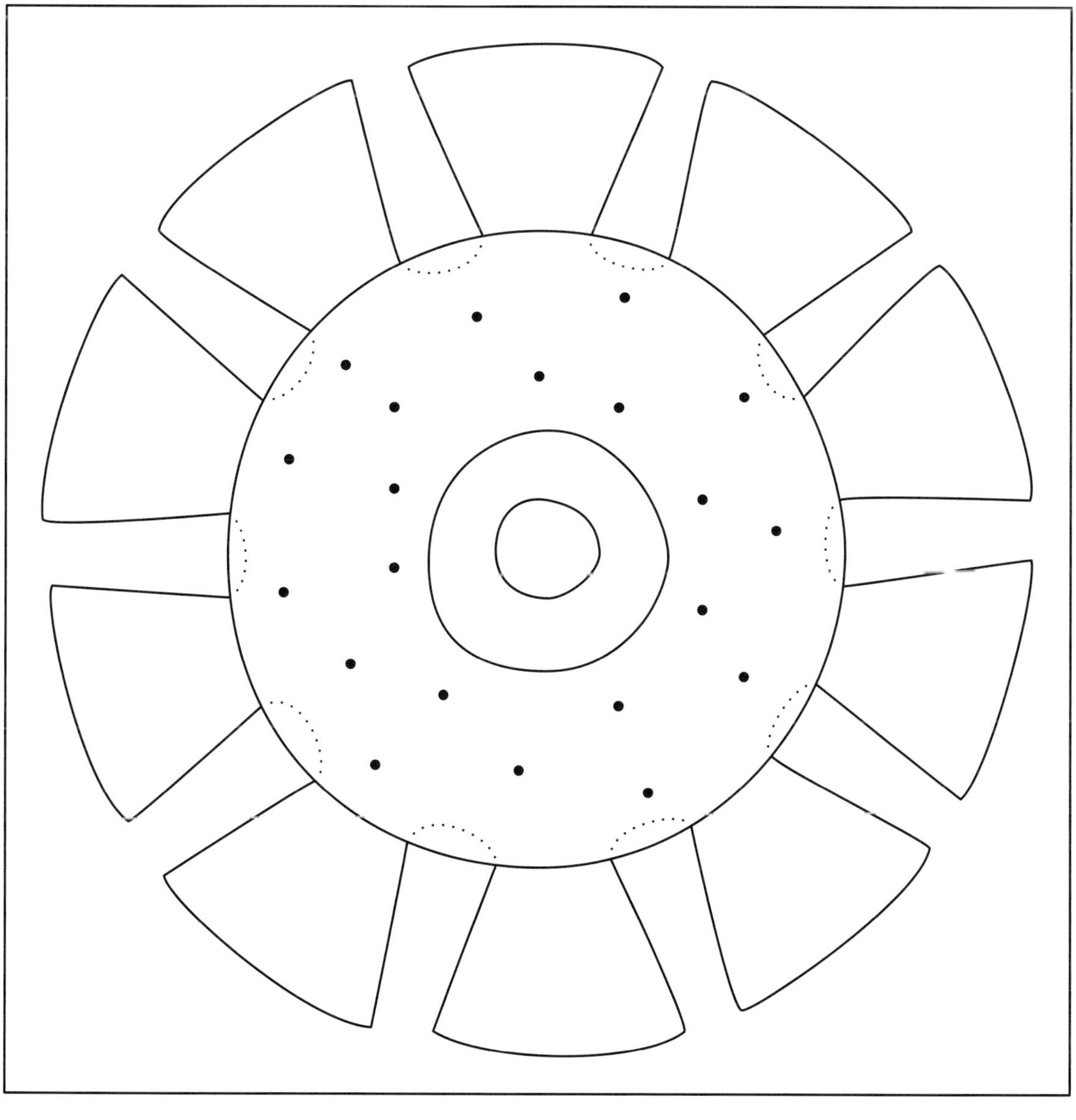

ASTER

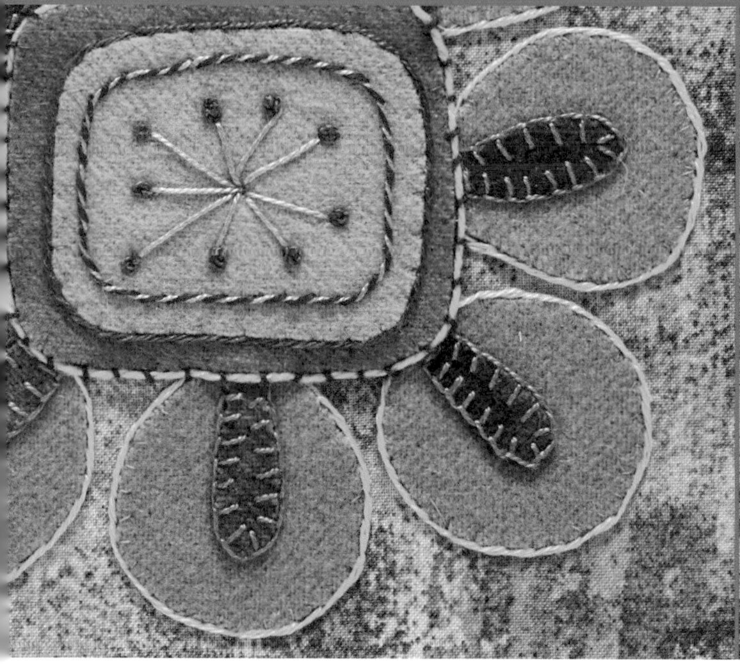

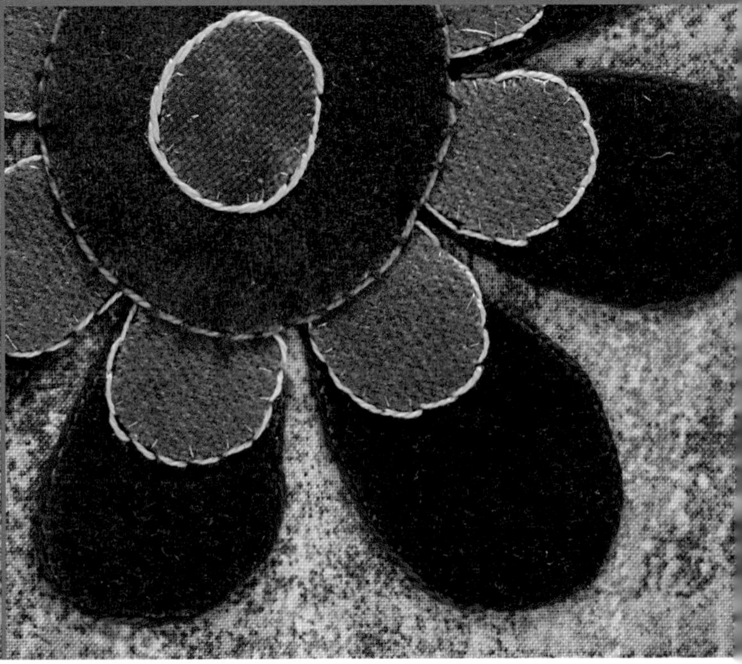

SPLATTER FLOWER

EMMA

About the Author

KIM SCHAEFER began sewing at an early age and was quilting seriously by the late 1980s. Her early quilting career included designing and producing small quilts for craft shows and shops across the country. In 1996, Kim founded Little Quilt Company, a pattern company focused on designing a variety of small, fun-to-make projects.

In addition to designing quilt patterns, Kim is a best-selling author for C&T Publishing. She also designs fabric for Andover Fabrics, Inc. Kim lives with her family in southeastern Wisconsin.

Follow Kim on social media:

WEBSITE: littlequiltcompany.com

(Be sure to check out Kim's fabric lines and products links for Kim's entire collection of patterns, books, and fabrics!)

FACEBOOK: Little Quilt Company

(Visit the Facebook page for posts about new patterns, books, and fabrics and an occasional peek at Kim's latest work!)

Also by Kim Schaefer:

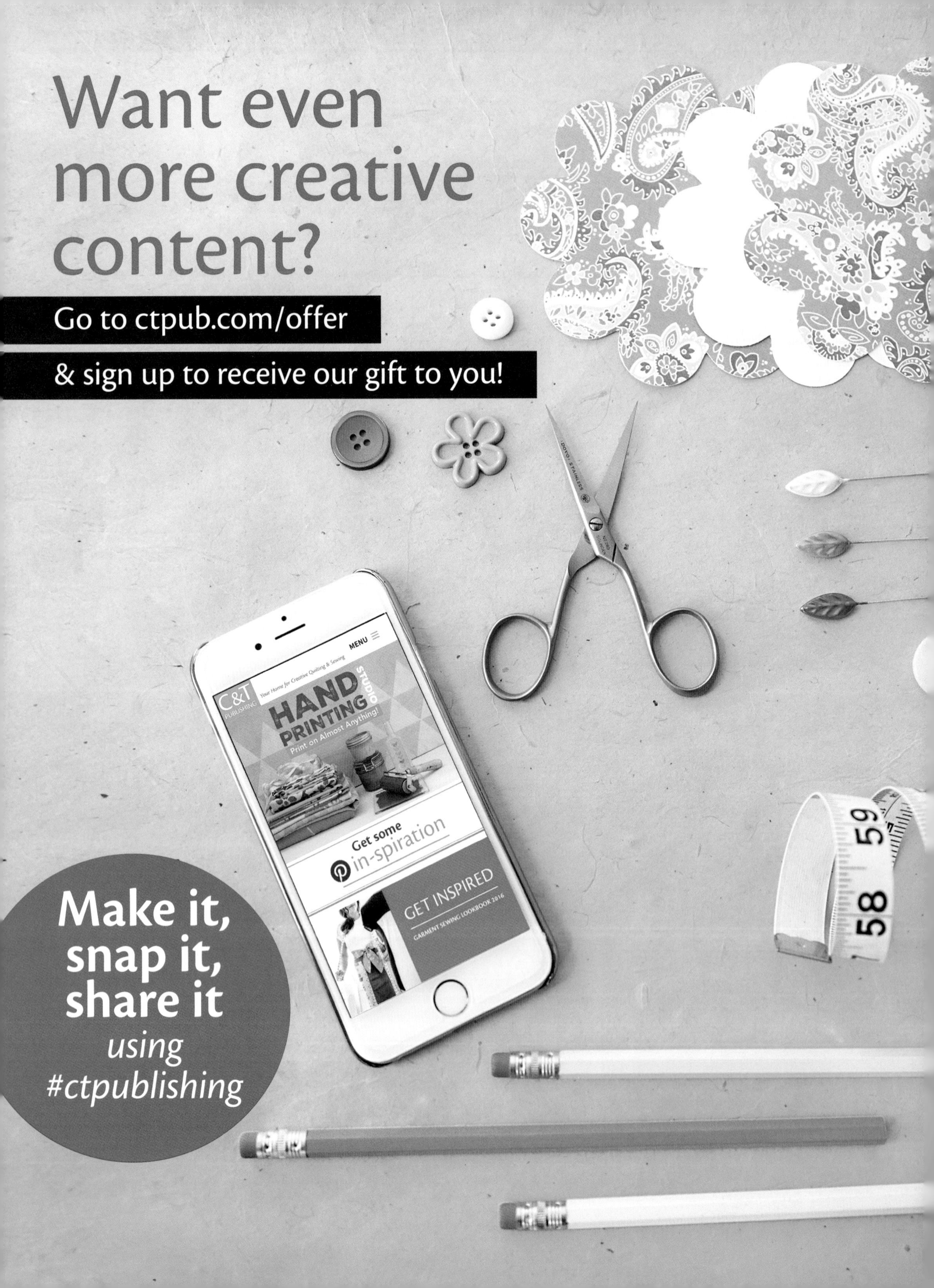
Want even more creative content?
Go to ctpub.com/offer
& sign up to receive our gift to you!
Make it, snap it, share it
using
#ctpublishing
MENU
C&T PUBLISHING
Your Home for Creative Quilting & Sewing
HAND PRINTING STUDIO
Print on Almost Anything!
Get some in-spiration
GET INSPIRED
GARMENT SEWING LOOKBOOK 2016